D0680664

# Sweet & Simple Moments with God

# Sweet & Simple Moments with God

## Kim Newlen

**TYNDALE**
**MOMENTUM**

*An Imprint of*
*Tyndale House Publishers, Inc.*

Visit Tyndale online at www.tyndale.com.

Visit Tyndale Momentum online at www.tyndalemomentum.com.

*Tyndale Momentum*, the Tyndale Momentum logo, *The One Year*, and *One Year* are registered trademarks of Tyndale House Publishers, Inc. The One Year logo is a trademark of Tyndale House Publishers, Inc. Tyndale Momentum is an imprint of Tyndale House Publishers, Inc.

*Sweet and Simple Moments with God*

Copyright © 2013 by Kim Newlen. All rights reserved.

Adapted from *The One Year Sweet and Simple Moments with God Devotional* by Tyndale House Publishers under ISBN 978-1-4143-7332-4. First printing by Tyndale House Publishers, Inc., in 2013.

Cover and interior line art copyright © vip2807/Dollar Photo Club. All rights reserved.

Author photograph by Wendell Powell Studio © 2012. All rights reserved.

Designed by Beth Sparkman

Edited by Erin K. Marshall and Bonne Steffen

Unless otherwise indicated, all Scripture quotations are taken from the *Holy Bible*, New Living Translation, copyright © 1996, 2004, 2007, 2013 by Tyndale House Foundation. Used by permission of Tyndale House Publishers, Inc., Carol Stream, Illinois 60188. All rights reserved.

Scripture quotations marked NIV are taken from the Holy Bible, *New International Version*,® *NIV*.® Copyright © 1973, 1978, 1984, 2011 by Biblica, Inc.® (Some quotations may be from the previous NIV edition, copyright © 1984.) Used by permission. All rights reserved worldwide.

Scripture quotations marked KJV are taken from the *Holy Bible*, King James Version.

Scripture quotations marked NKJV are taken from the New King James Version.® Copyright © 1982 by Thomas Nelson, Inc. Used by permission. All rights reserved.

Scripture quotations marked NASB are taken from the New American Standard Bible,® copyright © 1960, 1962, 1963, 1968, 1971, 1972, 1973, 1975, 1977, 1995 by The Lockman Foundation. Used by permission.

ISBN 978-1-4964-1162-4 (LeatherLike)

Printed in India

| 22 | 21 | 20 | 19 | 18 | 17 | 16 |
|----|----|----|----|----|----|----|
| 7  | 6  | 5  | 4  | 3  | 2  | 1  |

# Introduction

Dear Sweet Reader,

I wish you could see my so-excited face as I share with you this simple, sweet devotional. It's really not the words I am excited about sharing—it is the *Lord*, our Creator, the one true God, who sent Jesus, His only Son, not only to save us from our sin, but also to give us a personal relationship with Himself now and forever.

I came to accept God's free gift of salvation in Christ at an early age, but I did not begin to grow in my love for Him through His Word until I was a young adult. I try to live life with no regrets, but I do regret that I did not plunge into reading His Word every day a lot sooner. Getting to know God has been the greatest adventure of my life! The wildest thing is that the more difficult life is at times, the sweeter He becomes to me!

He is the same unchanging God who is still committed to His people—that's you and me in Christ. He loves us and forgives us. He helps us and changes us. He always has our backs and always has our best interests at heart. Spending time with Him and His Word is not on my "to-do" list but on my daily "want-to-do" list.

My hope and prayer is that we will all know and
grow in Christ together in the sweet days ahead.

His,

*Kim* ☀️

BSSYP (Be Sweet & Say Your Prayers)

SP (Sweet Pea): I know it is not fashionable to talk
about yourself, but it is in the spirit of Psalm 66:16—
His Spirit—that I share these simple devotions with you.
"Come and listen, all you who fear God, and I will tell
you what he did for me."

*How precious are your thoughts about me, O God.*

*They cannot be numbered! I can't even count them;*

*they outnumber the grains of sand!*

PSALM 139:17-18

# Sweet Tooth
# for God's Word

*How sweet your words taste to me; they are sweeter than honey.* Psalm 119:103

I have a confession to make. I have a big sweet tooth. If I had to point a finger at the culprit, I'd have a doughnut hanging there. Yes, it's true. Doughnuts are to blame.

When I was growing up, our family went to the beach every summer, and in the mornings my early-bird dad would go to the local doughnut shop and buy fresh ones hot off the conveyor belt for us. It was really a sweet "special delivery."

When we'd get home from vacation, we would beg Mama to make homemade doughnuts. She obliged us on a regular basis by deep-frying canned biscuits. She used a plastic bottle cap as her doughnut-hole cutter. We could choose chocolate or vanilla icing for her home-made delicacies, and she would slather it on and we would scarf them down! My mom fried the doughnut holes, too, which were my favorite because I could dip them in icing, covering the entire pastry.

I'm not a doughnut-a-day person anymore, but every now and then I buy the little powdered-sugar doughnuts to go with my coffee and Bible in the morning. In the same way I developed a craving for doughnuts, my sweet tooth for God's Word developed by repetition. When I actually began to read the Bible on a daily basis, His words became sweeter and sweeter as I interacted with Him each day through its pages.

As humans, we long for food that tastes good to us. We crave things that are pleasing to the taste, flavors we can savor for a while. And we love our sweets! In Bible times honey was the sweetest substance on earth.

In today's verse from Psalm 119, the psalmist craved the sweetness of the Lord's promises and instructions. In fact, for 176 verses, he cannot say enough about the value of God's Word.

Enjoy your sweet time with the Lord, indulging daily. His Word provides a sweet sustenance you and I cannot live without.

. . . . . . . . . .

RELISH THE SWEETNESS OF GOD'S WORD.
READ PSALM 119 AND WRITE DOWN A VERSE
OR TWO THAT SPEAK TO YOUR HEART.

# Our Father Always Knows Best

*[Jesus] never sinned, nor ever deceived anyone.*
1 Peter 2:22

Have you ever gotten something in the mail that says you have won a prize? My first "free prize" experience was in high school. Several days after a big fair came to our small hometown, I received a letter saying I had won a trip to Florida.

I couldn't contain my excitement. My dad came into the kitchen to find out what was causing all the commotion. When I showed him the letter, he said quietly, "Kim, this is a gimmick. There's a catch."

"No, Dad, I'm sure this is real." I didn't want to think that I had been tricked. Dad advised me to call some of my friends who had gone to the fair with me and had entered their names into the drawing for free prizes. I was ready to prove my dad wrong, so I got on the phone. Of course, Dad was right. All of my friends had "won" too! I was extremely disappointed.

My wise earthly father knew best about that so-called "free" prize. What's more, our heavenly Father knows and sees everything, more than we can imagine. All the more reason to trust Him.

We can know for sure that in all things, in all circumstances, and in all situations our heavenly Father speaks truth. He always knows best and never tricks us. We don't have to enter a raffle or a drawing to receive the greatest prize ever—eternal life with Him. God arranged for all of us to receive that free gift through His Son, Jesus Christ. All we need to do is ask and receive. It's the best thing we could ever hope to possess.

. . . . . . . . . .

WHAT A DAILY COMFORT IT IS THAT OUR FATHER
KNOWS BEST. WHAT QUESTION DO YOU NEED CLEAR
TRUTH ABOUT TODAY? HE ANSWERS IN HIS WORD.

# God Is Rich!

*God is so rich in mercy, and he loved us so much,*
*that even though we were dead because of our sins,*
*he gave us life when he raised Christ from the dead.*
*(It is only by God's grace that you have been saved!)*
Ephesians 2:4-5

God is rich in everything! And if you're His child, then so are you! How's that for good news in our struggling economy?

It's true. God's riches are vast and uncountable, and they all belong to His children. Those who love Him as Savior and Lord have all the benefits as heirs, and we can claim many parts of our inheritance today.

He makes His children rich in mercy, loaded with His kindness, wealthy in compassion, overflowing in grace, abundantly forgiven, and invested with hope. His affluence cannot be measured. We cannot fathom the lavishness of His love for us.

God is so magnificent and infinite, and we are so puny and poor. In His richness, He became poor for our sakes. He did not have to. Right now we can lay hold of all the riches He is pouring out upon us and trust that He will forever overflow those to us because He is inexhaustible. His wealth of wisdom, mercy, grace, love, and truth—everything good and right and pure and lovely—is ours through Christ. Because He loves us, He cannot help but give us His best.

Even though shoestring budgets are becoming the norm in our economy, God never operates on one. He doesn't skimp and never shortchanges us or withholds Himself from us. He never has to pinch and scrape and save to keep His resources from running out.

As I list His riches off the top of my head, my heart starts racing with joy. My heart can hardly hold His wealth, but I can be thankful that every day He's growing my heart larger to hold more of Himself.

. . . . . . . . . .

NO MATTER WHAT YOUR BANK ACCOUNT HOLDS TODAY, YOU ARE WEALTHY BY GOD'S KINGDOM STANDARDS IF YOU ARE HIS CHILD. ASK HIM FOR MORE OF HIMSELF TODAY. NOW TAKE THAT TO THE BANK!

## Loading Up the Carts

*Listen to my voice in the morning, LORD.*
*Each morning I bring my requests to you*
*and wait expectantly.* Psalm 5:3

When I go to the grocery store, I always—and I am
not exaggerating—*always* get more than what is on my
list! This habit is my attempt to follow my sweet friend
Sarah's advice to try something new every time I go to
the store. Plus, I'll often see an item I need for a particular recipe that I forgot to put on my list.

In the same way, when I go to God's Word each
morning with my grocery list of requests for His help,
His strength, His courage, and His patience for the day,
I always get more than I came for! God is so big, yet
so personal. The biggest supermarket we could envision
cannot begin to hold all of His awesome character
qualities, but He stocks them up in our hearts.

As we read His Word, our finite minds are capable
of processing only a glimpse of who He is. He, on the
other hand, knows our every thought and request before
we do. He supplies our every need, even if we have
not revealed the exact list of all that's crammed in our
heavy hearts.

What are some of His character qualities that He

loves to load up in our hearts! Let's list some of them.
He is:

- our Friend
- our Rescuer
- our Savior
- our Forgiver
- our Protector
- compassionate
- loving
- merciful

The list goes on and on—and on and on! No matter
how much we fill up on Him, the price at the check-
out is always the same—free! We never have to worry
about having enough funds to cover the cost of all He
gives us because He took care of our account long ago
through Jesus.

• • • • • • • • • •

WHAT OTHER ATTRIBUTES OF GOD CAN YOU
THINK OF? JOT DOWN HOW GOD SPIRITUALLY
NOURISHES YOU BECAUSE OF WHO HE IS.

## 5

# Confessions of a Leaner

*Come close to God, and God will come close to you.*
James 4:8

As much as I'd like to, I can't hide it: I'm a leaner. I am always being caught in the act by my family and friends who are the embarrassed recipients of my natural inclination. I stopped counting the number of times my daughter, Kali, has said in a public place, "Mom, you're leaning on me." I was oblivious! My "problem" is that I love to be close to people. Growing up, when I was walking anywhere with my friends—down the sidewalk, in the mall—they would be victims each and every time. I would just be brushing a shoulder!

Being in close proximity to people I love is how God made me. When I speak at churches or to women's groups, I ask if I can be as close to the women as possible. My husband, Mark, is the exact opposite. He needs some room, some sweet space! It's not just because he's tall; it's his reserved personality. Can you see why we're definitely a match made in heaven?

Naturally, I love leaning (pun intended!) toward the truth of today's verse. I can relate to it so well. It's comforting to know that our awesome God revels in our company. How amazing is that?

If you're thinking, *Kim, I'm too busy. I don't really have time to draw close to God*, here's what I would say: If you are reading this right now, you are actually being still for a moment. You are drawing close to God. Since God is the Word, we come close to Him by listening to what He has to say. As you meditate on His Word, you are leaning on Him.

Lean in, listen, and learn from God. Listen to others who love and lean on Him too. We can share this wonderful truth with those who do not know there is Someone they can lean on every day.

. . . . . . . . . .

### WHAT HAS GOD TAUGHT YOU RECENTLY AS YOU'VE LEANED ON HIM? FIND SOMEONE WHO NEEDS TO HEAR HOW GOD CAME CLOSE TO YOU.

# Grasping His Unfathomable Ways

*"My thoughts are nothing like your thoughts," says the
LORD. "And my ways are far beyond anything you could
imagine. For just as the heavens are higher than the
earth, so my ways are higher than your ways and my
thoughts higher than your thoughts."* Isaiah 55:8-9

I want to soak in this encouragement from God for
a minute with you. We each have a lot of our own
thoughts and our own ways, don't we? Our minds
process countless ideas every day—some we speak and,
thankfully, many we leave unspoken.

I have no idea how many thoughts on average run
through a person's mind each day. We definitely have
our individual ways of processing concepts and accom-
plishing things. In the simplest duties of daily life—
from squeezing the toothpaste tube from the bottom,
the top, or the middle to washing our hair every day or
a couple of times a week—our idiosyncrasies are many
and varied. And those examples don't even begin to
touch on the deeper issues of life!

It is mind-boggling that God not only knows my
every thought and my every way, but He knows yours,
too, and those of every living creature. Yet He is so

personal to each of His children. He knows everything that will pass through our minds and how our choices will affect us. He wants the very best for each of us and understands each of our unique dreams—and in every way His are higher.

The more I read about God and His thoughts and ways in His Word, the more *He gets bigger* and I grow smaller. How thrilling! Let's take another peek at some of His ways that we know for sure.

God's way is perfect. All the LORD's promises prove true.  Psalm 18:30

The way of the LORD is a stronghold to those with integrity.  Proverbs 10:29

Accept the way God does things, for who can straighten what he has made crooked?  Ecclesiastes 7:13

· · · · · · · · · · ·

KNOWING THE LORD'S UNFATHOMABLE WAYS, WHY WOULD WE SETTLE FOR LESS? TODAY LET ANY CONFUSION AND QUESTIONS FADE AS HIS HIGHER WAYS BECOME YOUR DESIRE!

# Pay It Upward

*These righteous ones will reply, "Lord, when did we ever
see you hungry and feed you? Or thirsty and give you
something to drink? Or a stranger and show you hospitality?
Or naked and give you clothing? When did we ever see
you sick or in prison and visit you?" And the King will say,
"I tell you the truth, when you did it to one of the least of
these my brothers and sisters, you were doing it to me!"*

Matthew 25:37-40

You've heard the term "pay it forward." But today's
verses make me want to "pay it upward!"

When we feed hungry people, give thirsty people
something to drink, show hospitality to a stranger,
provide clothing, or visit sick people or prisoners, we're
ministering to Jesus as well as to those in need.

Throughout the Gospels, Jesus tells us how to live.
*Gospel* means "good news," and Jesus Himself is Good
News! In some Bibles, the words of Jesus are printed
in red ink (it always looks pink to me). Every word in
Matthew 25 is red! When we read this chapter, it's like
we are sitting with the followers who were hearing Jesus
in person.

These verses are truly an invitation to love. Those
who know Jesus understand that His love for the

downtrodden is so great that He identifies Himself with them in order to impress on His listeners the value of serving them.

Jesus' way of service is not burdensome to us. It truly is a joy to reach out to others with the love of Christ, particularly those who suffer in this life. We can imagine His smile of compassion and hope each time we share His mercy and thoughtfulness, each time we purposefully open our eyes to look for those who need His love.

When we live to give, we not only pay it forward on a horizontal, earthly level, but we also pay it upward to Jesus. Do for Him by doing for others because He has done so much for us.

* * * * * * * * * *

CHOOSE ONE SIMPLE WAY TO SHARE GOD'S BLESSING WITH SOMEONE TODAY. DON'T TELL ANYONE—JUST DO IT AND PAY IT UPWARD.

# BSSYP

*Oh, that my actions would consistently reflect your decrees!*
Psalm 119:5

It truly is the little things in life repeated over and over that make the most lasting impressions. Consistency is crucial for connecting with people in a way that stirs love and warmth and builds trust in a relationship's stability. Consistency explains how family traditions *become* traditions.

Throughout our home—on license plates, art, and a mirror—the acronym BSSYP is on display. You see, when I went off to college, the first letter I received from home was written and addressed by my precious mother. My daddy had scribbled BSSYP in the upper left-hand corner of the envelope, along with a smiley face. For the life of me, I couldn't figure out what it meant. I was so homesick that I called home and said, "Daddy, what is that BSSYP?"

He replied, "Sugar, it is what I've told you all your life: Be Sweet & Say Your Prayers."

For over twenty-five years until the day he died, Daddy consistently wrote BSSYP on every package or piece of mail from home. More than merely scrawling letters, my father's actions consistently reflected a parent's love. Mom's too—he'd say she did all the hard work! Those five letters have become a legacy that my own daughter surely will pass on to generations after her. In fact, my first text from Kali, away at college, closed with BSSYP.

I long to tell everyone I know to be consistent in the small things. They can grow to leave legacies later in life. Our actions will reflect God's desires if we are giving Christ full access to our hearts.

. . . . . . . . . . .

ASK THE LORD TO HELP YOU BSSYP . . . AND TO BE CONSISTENT IN THE LITTLE BIG THINGS!

## 9

# Basking in the Son's Rays

*Jesus spoke to the people once more and said,
"I am the light of the world. If you follow me, you
won't have to walk in darkness, because you will
have the light that leads to life." John 8:12*

You would be laughing if you could see me right now.
It is early morning, I am in my favorite lightweight long
robe, and I just sat down to read my Bible. It's too cold
to go outside for devotions, so I am doing the next best
thing—sitting near the window. What's so funny is that
I had to get up and put on my sun visor to read my
Bible in the house! I could have moved from my sunny
spot, but I did not want to because the sun's warmth
makes me realize that God's Son, Jesus Christ, is sending
His rays in my direction.

*Shine on me, Lord. I need Your Sonshine!*

Christ is comfort. Christ is light. As I am soaking in
physical warmth and light from the sun, I long to soak
in the One who created these necessities. I long to allow
the Son to illumine His way for me this day, this hour—
all day and night and the next until I reach heaven,
where there is no darkness!

The rays really are bright, and I briefly consider
whether I need to get sunscreen. I'm so glad that when

18

it comes to getting burned by the heat of my sins, I have the 100++ percent protection of *Sonscreen*.

*Lord, You are my shield from sin. You see me without sin's damage, made perfect through the death of Christ, Your Son, on the cross.*

I probably should get out of the sun before it burns me, but I never need to limit my time in the direct presence of the Son, and neither do you. In fact, the more we soak Him up, the more we'll glow with His Sonshine lighting us from the inside out. Jesus is our SPF 100++ (Son Protection Forever).

• • • • • • • • • • •

YOU AND I MAY BE FACING SOME DARK SITUATIONS, SO LET JESUS' WORDS SHINE INTO OUR HEARTS. WHEN WE FOLLOW HIM, WE HAVE THE PROTECTION OF SONSCREEN AND THE SON'S RAYS. HIS SPIRIT PRODUCES THE GLOW!

# *You Look Very Fine*

*The LORD doesn't see things the way you see
them. People judge by outward appearance,
but the LORD looks at the heart.* 1 Samuel 16:7

Whenever I ask my daughter or husband how I look
and they reply, "You look just fine," I want to head right
back to my closet and start over! Of course, I usually
do not have enough time for that, so I leave the house
looking "just fine."

What is meant by "fine" anyway? My children's dictionary, which I prefer to use for simplicity, defines *fine*
as "very well or healthy." All I can think of is that I don't
look sick and that because I look "healthy," people think
I've gained weight!

Our loving God tells us plainly that although we
see outward appearances and do not see the heart, He
does see the heart, and that's what really matters. What
a beautiful truth! He sees the good, the bad, and the
ugly in our hearts, regardless of the state of our outward
appearance. Beautiful to Him is quite different from the
world's definition of beauty.

He sees my heart when it isn't so fine because I've
failed, yet He knows I want to please Him. He knows
my weak heart is made of dust but it still beats for Him.

He knows I love Him and want to be obedient until my heart stops beating on this earth, when I finally will see Him face to face. That happens not because I look fine, but because I *am* very fine—perfect, actually—in Jesus Christ. You, too, are very fine—perfect, actually—in Jesus Christ, whether you feel or look "just fine" or not.

It is encouraging to know that even though God sees and knows everything about us, He still has plans for us that are a lot more than just fine!

* * * * * * * * * * *

THANK GOD THAT HE MADE OUR HEARTS
FOREVER PERFECT IN JESUS CHRIST.
"JUST FINE" WILL HARDLY DO!

## 11

# Source of All Comfort

*Share each other's burdens, and in this way
obey the law of Christ.* Galatians 6:2

Think back to the last time you were truly uncomfortable. Perhaps you are experiencing discomfort right now. I imagine you are just like me. You, too, long for freedom from your distress as quickly as possible.

When I am uncomfortable, I want the pain to stop hurting my heart and my body. As I've said before, if I had to choose, I would take physical pain over emotional pain. I would rather lose a breast than a child; I cannot even imagine that kind of emotional pain.

But the God of all comfort (2 Corinthians 1:3-4) does more than just imagine our pain; He enters into it with us. There is not one thing that we feel that the God of all comfort has not felt first. "Since [Jesus] himself has gone through suffering and testing, he is able to help us when we are being tested" (Hebrews 2:18).

I take great comfort in the truth of today's verse. When I try to ease the burdens of others, I send Band-Aid notes to people who are hurting. I always feel inadequate to know what to say. My heart hurts for them, but I realize that I cannot make their pain go away. However, I know for a fact that God will comfort them in ways that only He can, and He can use even my simple steps to comfort my hurting friends more deeply than I can.

One way to partner with God in offering His comfort is to pray for others every time God brings them to mind. We can also take them a meal, offer to run an errand, or let someone know they are loved with a hug. Once a sweet neighbor, Judy, brought me a package of chocolate-covered strawberries from the produce section of the "healthy" store. They were so beautiful and so tasty. Her sweet gift touched me so much that I went to the same store to purchase the same gift for someone else who was suffering, to let her know she was loved.

· · · · · · · · · ·

LET GOD COMFORT YOU TODAY THROUGH HIS WORD,
AND USE IT TO SHARE SOMEONE ELSE'S BURDEN TOO!

# Read the Directions

*Trust in the LORD with all your heart; do not depend on your own understanding. Seek his will in all you do, and he will show you which path to take.* Proverbs 3:5-6

I didn't develop a taste for coffee until I was an adult visiting my sweet mama. She and my younger sister, Shawn, would drink it together in the mornings, and since I didn't want to miss anything, I joined in. The more coffee I had from my mother's favorite china cups with the thin rims she loved, the more I liked it.

When I returned home after that first trip, I knew I had to learn to make coffee myself. After making the rounds at various coffee shops, I decided on my favorite brand and was delighted that I could also purchase it at the grocery store.

But for some reason when I made it at our home, it never came close to how it tasted in the coffee shops or at my mother's! I changed coffee pots, changed filters, and even changed creamers. I tried adding more boiling water. Nothing worked.

I finally figured out where my brewing skills went wrong (although I am almost too embarrassed to admit it). I never read the directions on the side of the package that gave the proper measurements for the water and the coffee. I completely skipped them and foolishly wasted a lot of coffee and filters.

When I finally came to my senses, I said to the Lord at my kitchen counter, "I do not want to do this kind of thing with You, Lord. Not ever. I want to follow Your directions laid out in Your Word, day by day, moment by moment."

. . . . . . . . . .

BE SURE TO READ GOD'S DIRECTIONS IN HIS WORD— WITH OR WITHOUT A CUP OF COFFEE—KEEPING HIS INSTRUCTIONS HANDY FOR LIVING FAITHFULLY. THAT'S REALLY SOMETHING TO SIP ON.

# What Is a
# Sweet Monday?

*That is what the Scriptures mean when they
say, "No eye has seen, no ear has heard, and no
mind has imagined what God has prepared for
those who love him."* 1 Corinthians 2:9

In 1995, I was a young mother busy with our daughter, Kali, at home while my husband, Mark, was at his
job at school. At times, I felt isolated and longed for
the company of other women. I knew I couldn't be the
only woman feeling this way . . . and I knew Jesus! So I
decided that with God's help, I would open our home
the first Monday night of the month for an hour and
a half to any woman who would come—neighbors,
church friends, acquaintances, women of all ages and
stages of life.

Since our household income had been signifi-
cantly reduced when I stopped teaching, I called the
get-together "Sweet Monday, Women's Socials on a
Shoestring . . . Tied to a Generous God." I served
a simple dessert (full of fat and sugar), decaf coffee,
and candy to go along with the theme. Because
God promises that His Word never returns void
(Isaiah 55:11, KJV), I shared a five-minute gospel

26

message to point us all to Christ as the one and only lasting Sweetener of life!

The night before that first Sweet Monday, I dreamed that I was sitting on the front porch in a rocking chair, waiting and waiting for someone to come. Not one woman showed up! It was a terrible dream, but thankfully it wasn't what actually happened. The next night the living room was crowded, and new women continued to come month after month, year after year.

What about you? We can all have a Sweet Monday any day of the week by reaching out to another woman for Christ, one sweet invitation at a time! If we who have Christ living inside us aren't connecting other women to Him, who will? Let's invite women into our lives, into our homes, and into our churches by faith!

* * * * * * * * * *

EXTEND AN INVITATION TO A WOMAN THIS WEEK FOR COFFEE OR TEA. IT MAY LEAD TO A REGULAR BIBLE STUDY OR SWEET MONDAY IN YOUR HOME. BUT START WITH ALLOWING THE HOLY SPIRIT TO ENCOURAGE HER THROUGH HIS LIFE IN YOU.

# God Watches Over Us

*He will not let you stumble; the one who watches over you will not slumber. Indeed, he who watches over Israel never slumbers or sleeps. The LORD himself watches over you! The LORD stands beside you as your protective shade. The sun will not harm you by day, nor the moon at night. The LORD keeps you from all harm and watches over your life. The LORD keeps watch over you as you come and go, both now and forever.* Psalm 121:3-8

How many times have you and I told young children to look both ways before they cross the street? And how many times have we told a teenager in the driver's seat to be sure to check in both directions before pulling out into an intersection?

We'd like to be able to always watch over those we love, but we have to trust that when it matters most, they will act on the wisdom they've been taught. Fortunately, we can trust God to be on guard over them at all times, even when we cannot be with them. Sometimes we feel even more peace knowing that He is caring for those we love than we feel knowing that He's watching over us.

Psalm 121 is a short and sweet reminder that God is at attention in our lives 24/7, wherever we are, whatever we are doing, in and out of our households, from the mundane to the exciting, the ordinary to the extraordinary—whatever, wherever, God is watching over you and me!

If you have your Bible handy, turn to Psalm 121 and notice that in eight verses the psalmist declares six times that God helps, watches over, protects, and stands beside you and me. At the beginning of the psalm we are on the lookout for God: "I look up to the mountains— does my help come from there? My help comes from the LORD" (verses 1-2). One of life's most abiding comforts comes from knowing that even if *we* are not on the lookout moment by moment, God is always watching over us.

. . . . . . . . . .

JOIN ME IN WATCHING AND WAITING ON HIM DAILY! THANK GOD FOR HIS HEDGE OF PROTECTION AROUND YOU IN CHRIST.

# Got Hope?

*Even Christ didn't live to please himself. As the*
*Scriptures say, "The insults of those who insult you,*
*O God, have fallen on me." Such things were written in*
*the Scriptures long ago to teach us. And the Scriptures*
*give us hope and encouragement as we wait patiently*
*for God's promises to be fulfilled.* Romans 15:3-4

Got hope? If only having hope were as easy as getting a
milk mustache—one taste and we'd be branded with it.

Sometimes it feels as if hope is hard to come by. But
hope in Christ is readily available every minute. God
wants us to drink deeply of it, believing that hope can
never be wiped away! He tells us that the Scriptures,
such as today's verses written by the apostle Paul, give us
hope and encouragement. Since the Scriptures are God's
actual words to us, it is His personal encouragement and
hope that we are receiving.

This hope is designed to permeate our souls so that
even under the most dire circumstances, it strengthens
us and the glory of God shines through us so others will
see that He is the Source of our hope.

If we can't seem to find hope right now, we need to
ask ourselves how long it's been since we last opened the
Scriptures. I'm not talking about looking up something

for an assignment or to prepare for a Bible study—just purposely being still, ready to listen to God's voice.

God tells us plainly through the Scriptures that we can have hope! He knows how much we need it in our anxiety-filled lives. He assures us over and over again that every promise He makes will come true.

You and I have probably spent a lot of time in the "waiting room" of life, hoping for greater hope, waiting to hear a word from Him. When hope is our companion in the waiting room, those moments can be a joy, privilege, comfort, and exciting adventure while we thrive in His presence!

. . . . . . . . . .

## WRITE "I WILL HOPE IN CHRIST ALONE" ON A CARD OR STICKY NOTE AND PUT IT SOMEPLACE WHERE YOU CAN SEE IT OFTEN.

# Southern Spanish

*I have summoned you by name;*
*you are mine.* Isaiah 43:1, NIV

Have you ever tried speaking Spanish with a southern accent? Even though I took two years of Spanish in high school and performed well on the written tests, I could never quite get the hang of speaking Spanish aloud—especially in front of other people! Because I did so well on the written tests, I was placed in the more advanced second-year class at Erskine College. Oh my, I was totally unprepared for that!

*Lost* does not even begin to describe the inadequacy I felt Monday, Wednesday, and Friday for two whole weeks! Our professor spoke Spanish fluently and very fast the whole class. We even played Spanish bingo, but not one square on my card was ever filled! When our teacher called the roll in our special Spanish names, I never uttered a sound (although I desperately wanted to scream "Adios!" because I couldn't even understand my Spanish name being called).

Sheer fear and embarrassment held me back from saying anything at first, but I finally made an appointment to see my professor after two weeks had passed. I admitted to her how lost I was. She told me she had assumed I had dropped the class. Since I had never responded when she called me by my Spanish name, she had marked me absent the six times I was actually there.

Once again, God used a life experience to help me appreciate that He summons me by name. The one and only true God, Creator of everything and the God infinitely involved with His people every minute of every day, has called me by name. He has called you by name too.

He wants us to know that He has us covered for all eternity and that we will not be counted absent "when the roll is called up yonder," as the old hymn says, because we belong to Him in Jesus Christ if we have received Him by faith.

We may not understand some of our circumstances in this life, but we can rest assured that God fully understands us. He knows the unique language of our heart. He speaks whatever language we speak (including Southern) fluently, and He delights in helping us learn His language of love.

. . . . . . . . . . .

NO NAME GAMES WITH GOD! ASK HIM TO GIVE
YOU A GLIMPSE TODAY OF HIS PERSONAL CARE
FOR YOU, A CHILD HE LOVES TO CALL BY NAME.

# Our Mediator

*There is one God, and one mediator between God and men, the man Christ Jesus.* 1 Timothy 2:5, KJV

A few years ago a meteor shower was forecast in our area for the wee hours of the morning. Our family—complete with my sweet widowed mother, who was visiting—piled into the truck, drove out to the country, and watched the glorious sight in our sleeping bags, laid out in the bed of the pink truck.

It was quite a sight, but what I will remember most is heading for church the next morning. I usually keep candy in my pocketbook, in a dish in my foyer, or in my pink truck. I'm sure this habit is a result of my sweet dad's huge influence. He used to tuck candy in his pocket for my siblings and me when he arrived home from work. I carried this habit into our family, and we hardly ever got into my late daddy's truck that I inherited without having cute candy mints (with verses on them) handy. They were my daughter's favorite!

Well, as we sleepily drove to church the morning after the meteor shower, I pulled out a mint at my daughter's request, and she read, "There is one 'meteor' between God and men." What a wonderful opportunity to laugh and share about our only way to God—our Mediator—Jesus Christ.

Jesus being our Mediator is the sweetest Good News we will ever hear! We know God personally through the man Jesus Christ, who makes possible our relationship with the Creator and Ruler of everything. His Spirit in us guides us through life and helps us reflect Jesus' character to people all around us who need Him to mediate on their behalf too.

⬤ ⬤ ⬤ ⬤ ⬤ ⬤ ⬤ ⬤ ⬤ ⬤

THANK GOD TODAY FOR *THE MAN—OUR MEDIATOR, JESUS!* WRITE A NOTE OF GRATITUDE TO HIM TODAY; TELL HIM WHAT HIS LOVE MEANS TO YOU AND HOW YOU VALUE HIS ROLE AS MEDIATOR TO CONNECT YOU WITH YOUR HEAVENLY FATHER.

# My People

*They will be my people, and I will be their God, for they will return to me wholeheartedly.* Jeremiah 24:7

My sweet friend Faye was telling me about visiting her great-aunt in a nursing home. Her aunt was experiencing the effects of dementia, and she didn't recognize Faye. But then Faye's great-aunt said to her, "I know you are my people."

*My people.* Such a personal claim of belonging. It sounded so familiar to me, and God recalled to my mind that He refers to us as His people throughout Scripture. "My people" sounded like God speaking through Faye's great-aunt, and my heart was touched.

When God was directing Moses as His mouthpiece, God would tell him what to say to Pharaoh, and Moses would say it. Over and over Moses told Pharaoh that God said, "Let *My people* go!" How personal is that?

Even though He was speaking specifically to the Israelite nation in that instance, God adopts all believers in Christ as *His people* too. We are in God's immediate family, related to Him forever because of Jesus. Just as God claimed the Israelites, He claims us as His own. And like He did for them, God defends us. He is crazy about us and is always watching out for us as a capable Father.

If you're in God's family, you need to take courage in what God says about you: "You are *My people*!" We live in a hurting world where many people don't know they can be God's people too. We can introduce them to our heavenly Father and increase the joy at the family reunion in heaven!

• • • • • • • • • •

LET'S HEAR GOD SAY TO US TODAY IN CHRIST, "YOU ARE *MY PEOPLE*." WRITE A NOTE TO GOD ABOUT WHAT BEING A PART OF HIS FAMILY MEANS TO YOU. READ COLOSSIANS 3:12 TO SEE A LIST OF TRAITS OF GOD'S FAMILY MEMBERS.

# *Sweet Homework*

*God has given us this task of reconciling people to him.*
*For God was in Christ, reconciling the world to himself,*
*no longer counting people's sins against them. And he*
*gave us this wonderful message of reconciliation. So we*
*are Christ's ambassadors.* 2 Corinthians 5:18-20

What a sweet homework assignment we have as ambassadors for Christ! But what exactly does that assignment involve?

As Christ's ambassadors, we represent His name and Kingdom to the world. He chose us and appointed us to speak on His behalf to spread His message of salvation, love, and peace. When you and I joined the family of God by faith in Christ, He gave us full access to Himself, including 24/7 clearance to convene with Him. He is always in session to provide insight and wisdom for how best to accomplish His work.

He showers us with such gifts and privileges, too. It's as if we're both royalty and workers in His country, which is exactly what we are! We don't go around expecting to be introduced with trumpets and great pomp. Any position requires constant sweet homework behind the scenes before He places any of His children on the front lines.

He clearly tells us that our commitment involves sharing His wonderful message of reconciliation, which is the gospel, the Good News. We can be used by Him in a myriad of ways to take His Good News to others so that they can be reconciled to Him too. We all have the same task as ambassadors of Christ, but our roles will be as unique as each one of us! Some may sit at someone's bedside; others may write an e-mail. Some may travel great distances, and others may work from home. Still more will rescue the wounded and protect those in danger. All God's children are his ambassadors, offering God's truth and grace.

Most of all, as God's ambassadors we need to make sure we're conducting ourselves in a manner that honors Him as we extend the level of care He asks of us to those we serve. Only through our personal relationship with God in Christ will we be effective as His ambassadors.

* * * * * * * * * * * *

LET'S JOIN FORCES AND TAKE OUR AMBASSADORSHIP SERIOUSLY BY ABIDING IN CHRIST AND THEN CARRYING OUT OUR ASSIGNMENT FAITHFULLY.

# Sticky Friendships

*There are "friends" who destroy each other, but a real
friend sticks closer than a brother.* Proverbs 18:24

Friendships are one of God's richest blessings in life,
and I thank God for each of my friends. We've spilled
out so much laughter and so many tears together over
the years. Friends are true gifts, and I hope to bless them
with faithful friendship as well.

Stop and think for a minute about why we love
our earthly friends. Is it the ease with which we can call
them anytime, day or night? Is it the fact that before we
even mention a need, they have already taken care of it?
Or maybe they are just plain fun to be with.

Yet in our darkest days of overwhelming circumstances with no easy solutions, even though friends offer
welcome comfort, they can't always change our situation
for the better. Sometimes other priorities require their
attention; sometimes those we feel closest to move away,
and we long for friends who stick around whenever we
need them.

My sweet reader friend, each one of us has a Forever
Friend. Whatever our distressing circumstances or
heartaches, this Friend knows all about us and loves
us unconditionally. He is never busy, always available,

and always kind. He never moves away. He is the only Friend who promises (with power to follow through) that He will use all things for the good of His children in conforming us to Christ.

I hope and pray that you recognize Him as such a Friend and that you enjoy lots of time with Him. His name is Jesus, and He stays close forever. Our relationship with Him is one sticky friendship we cannot live without!

· · · · · · · · · ·

LET'S REMEMBER THAT GOD LONGS FOR ALL OF US TO KNOW HIM AS OUR VERY BEST FRIEND. LET'S ASK HIM TO HELP US OFFER A TASTE OF HIS FRIENDSHIP TO SOMEONE TODAY.

# A Done Deal

*I have written this to you who believe in the
name of the Son of God, so that you may
know you have eternal life.* 1 John 5:13

Sometimes in our Christian life, doubts set in, and we may feel that our faith isn't quite good enough. We may even think God wants to cancel His commitment to us because we have failed Him in a certain way or doubted or worried. Well, thank the Lord that we can relax about this one thing: faith in Christ is a done deal. There is no return policy, only opportunities for growth.

God wants each of us to trust Him to hold our lives and eternities securely. In His great love, grace, mercy, and kindness, He knows we will struggle and wonder if He is going to return us to the way we were, dead in our sin. Well, hallelujah, He will not!

In Christ, we are His and He is ours. The eternal deal He made for us lasts forever, which means that His presence and help are available to us every second.

Imagine living each moment trusting *fully* that He personally lavishes His grace and strength on you. He is a hands-on God, and He extends His grace to us when we sin and even when we fail to trust Him. He blesses faith that's as minuscule as a mustard seed (Luke 17:6), and He gives us more opportunities to grow in faith. He believes that we can learn to trust Him more, and instead of punishing us when we disobey, He grows us.

He dwells within us the moment we receive Him, and He wants us to live with the assurance that the exchange is complete and we have eternal life as well as His help during this earthly life.

How wonderful to celebrate every day knowing that God will not take back our relationship with Him.

· · · · · · · · · ·

THINK ABOUT THIS TRUTH OF ASSURANCE THE NEXT TIME YOU ARE RETURNING SOMETHING AT THE STORE. ONCE YOU'RE GOD'S, YOU'RE GOD'S FOR GOOD!

# 22

# Refreshed with Life-Giving Water

*O God, you are my God; I earnestly search for you.
My soul thirsts for you; my whole body longs for you
in this parched and weary land. Psalm 63:1*

Parched, weary, and thirsty. David was hiding in a desolate wilderness when he penned Psalm 63. He was in the wilderness of Judah, on the run from his rebellious son Absalom, who was trying to kill him.

I cannot imagine that particular wilderness situation, but I know what it feels like to be so thirsty that nothing will satisfy me but good ol' $H_2O$! Most of us don't have to stay thirsty very long. We can quickly quench our physical thirst. But when it comes to soul thirst, *nothing* will satisfy it but Jesus, our Living Water!

When we're in a "parched and weary" situation—the kind of wilderness experience that seems like it will never end, with circumstances that make us crave relief for ourselves or for those we love—we don't know how much longer we can last in the desert and wonder if help will ever arrive. Only the Lord Himself can meet us with His life-giving water and satisfy our deepest needs.

Let's look at David's Living Water bottle of relief that's found in Psalm 63:

Seek God. (verse 1)

Tell God we long for Him. (verse 1)

Remember good experiences with God and God's power and glory. (verse 2)

Praise God for His unfailing love. (verses 3-4)

Compliment God and praise Him some more. (verse 5)

Think about God when we can't sleep. (verse 6)

Remember God is our keeper and sing for joy. (verse 7)

Follow Him closely and recognize that His strong hand holds us securely. (verse 8)

Watch God protect us. (verses 9-10)

Rejoice in Him and show your trust by praising Him. (verse 11)

* * * * * * * * * *

TALK ABOUT AN ENERGIZING DRINK! DRINK HIM IN AND THEN FILL UP AGAIN. YOU WILL BE RENEWED AND REFRESHED BY ALL THAT HE OFFERS.

# Little Things Mean a Lot

*Well done, my good and faithful servant.* Matthew 25:21

I will never forget an early motherhood moment centered on our small kitchen table. I had been home full-time about a year after ending an almost-ten-year teaching career so that I could raise our baby. My husband, Mark, who is also a schoolteacher and coach, agreed with me on this *big* step of faith.

That particular summer day, I was attempting to add some color and cheer to our kitchen table. I couldn't buy anything, so I needed to be creative. I put out a fresh set of placemats, picked some dandelions from the yard, and placed them in a small vase at the center of the table. When the task was done, I got busy with something else. Then three-year-old Kali came into the kitchen, walked by the table, patted it with her sweet little hand, and said, "Pretty, Mommy. Pretty, Mommy." My heart swelled and tears came to my eyes as I breathed a quick "Thank You, Lord" for her precious affirmation that I had done well by adding His touch to our table.

Words of encouragement are so powerful. Anytime we look beyond our own interests and take an interest in others (Philippians 2:4), God is pleased! Our efforts reveal His Spirit at work inside of us.

When my young child said, "Pretty, Mommy," I heard God's voice echo in my mind, *Well done! Well done!* I sensed His pleasure. Even though He was the only One who witnessed that moment, I felt His encouragement.

. . . . . . . . . .

SOAK IN HIS WORDS TODAY, AND ACT ON THE THINGS THAT GOD STIRS IN YOUR HEART TO DO, NO MATTER HOW BIG OR SMALL THEY ARE. EXPERIENCE THE JOY THAT COMES FROM RESPONDING TO HIS PROMPTING.

## 24

# *Reminders*

*And now, O LORD, God of Israel, carry out the*
*additional promise you made to your servant David,*
*my father. For you said to him, "If your descendants*
*guard their behavior and faithfully follow my Law as*
*you have done, one of them will always sit on the throne*
*of Israel." Now, O LORD, God of Israel, fulfill this*
*promise to your servant David.* 2 Chronicles 6:16-17

How do you remind yourself of things you don't want
to forget? Maybe you're a list maker, and you keep a
pad of paper close by at all times. Maybe you've grown
attached to the calendar on your favorite handheld
device. Or maybe you're one of those rare people who
keeps all details carefully sorted in your head—if so,
I am truly impressed.

This passage serves as a timeless reminder about
God's promises. Solomon, David's son, had completed
his appointed task of building the Temple of the Lord,
furnishing it, and placing the Ark of the Lord's Covenant
in the sanctuary. The people offered songs of praise
and many sacrifices in thanksgiving to God. The whole
nation of Israel was there, and Solomon prayed for all
the people. King Solomon praised God for keeping His
promise that He made to Solomon's father, David.

I'm glad that God never needs reminders, but we can reaffirm our own faith by reminding *ourselves* in front of God of what He promises throughout His Word. Repeating His promises as we pray and worship Him can rally our faith.

    God's promises in Scripture give us courage to live with vibrant faith. Like Solomon, we can boldly "remind God" that we are counting on His continued faithfulness to us. We will see God proven true over and over again!

• • • • • • • • • •

WE NEED A DAILY REVIEW OF GOD'S FAITHFULNESS TO US. CHOOSE A COUPLE OF YOUR FAVORITE PROMISES AND REVIEW THEM WITH GOD. TELL HIM YOU BELIEVE HIS PROMISES AND YOU KNOW THEY'LL BE PROVEN TRUE!

# 25

# The Best Way of Life

*Let me show you a way of life that is best of all. . . .*
*Love is patient and kind. Love is not jealous or boastful*
*or proud or rude. It does not demand its own way.*
*It is not irritable, and it keeps no record of being*
*wronged. It does not rejoice about injustice but rejoices*
*whenever the truth wins out. Love never gives up, never*
*loses faith, is always hopeful, and endures through*
*every circumstance.* 1 Corinthians 12:31; 13:4-7

I *love* this *love* passage, but not because it makes me feel
like a loving person! In fact, it reminds me of where I fall
short in my relationships with people I really love. That's
especially true when I am struggling to forgive someone
I feel has wronged me in some way. I have to work hard
to keep myself from holding a grudge or fighting back.

I believe most of us have grown up thinking that the
concept of love is pretty simple and straightforward. You
meet someone, fall in love, and live happily ever after.
First Corinthians 13 explains the many components of
love, all characteristics of God, who loved us so much
that "he gave his one and only Son, so that everyone
who believes in him will not perish but have eternal life"
(John 3:16). Love isn't as simple as it seems. It isn't as
mushy as I always dreamed it would be. There's a lot of
work involved—but it's His best work.

God is the only One who demonstrates love perfectly. He keeps no record of wrongs. He is always patient with us and kind to us. God is always loving toward us, which means He never gives up on us, never loses faith in us, is always hopeful. He endures through every circumstance with us, and there have probably been some tough ones. God *is love*! Reading 1 Corinthians 13 sheds light on how much God has loved and forgiven us, and quickens our hearts to forgive others. Love is the best way because it's His way!

•  •  •  •  •  •  •  •  •  •

NEXT TIME YOU ARE STRUGGLING TO FORGIVE SOMEONE, READ 1 CORINTHIANS 13:4-7 AND ASK GOD TO GIVE YOU THE WORDS YOU NEED TO SAY.

# 26

# *Look What He Did*

*Come and listen, all you who fear God, and I
will tell you what he did for me.* Psalm 66:16

In case you haven't noticed, it is difficult for me *not* to
talk about God! I cannot seem to keep Him to myself.
I feel like I have blurted Him out on these pages.

But I am second-guessing myself right now because
my reflections are so personal, and I am worried about
what people will think. Is my concern because God's
Word is on every page and He is so precious, true, right,
good, instructive, and *perfect*? Or because His reputation
is of much greater concern than my own and I'm not
sure I can do it justice? Or is it because a few tiny words
on paper cannot begin to describe Him adequately?

Telling what He did for me is like a perpetual
run-on sentence: God *is* grace, love, mercy, strength,
redemption, ever-present, forgiving, glorious, honor-
able, perfect, complete, constant, assuring, kind, patient,
personal, encouraging, enduring, peaceful, just, righteous, light, consistent, holy, powerful, friendly, true,
comforting, caring, good, and on and on—forever and
ever and ever and ever! When I think about God's character, I reaffirm to myself some of the reasons I love to
talk about Him.

It is hard not to talk about such a great God, who is personal and who has saved me from sin so that I can wake up every day and face the future with hope and genuine gladness in my heart.

And you know what? Even in my feeble attempt just now to focus on Him, He has revealed the reason for my second-guessing: No words or expressions can touch His magnificence or how He deals with me with such love! I am accepting the fact that there are no words that truly glorify Him enough. But I'm going to spend my life offering Him my worship and praise and thanksgiving anyway! That is what He desires from each of us.

* * * * * * * * * *

BRAINSTORM FOR FIVE MINUTES AND WRITE A LIST OF WHAT GOD HAS DONE FOR YOU AND HOW HE SHOWS YOU HIS LOVE. "OUR HEART'S DESIRE IS TO GLORIFY YOUR NAME" (ISAIAH 26:8).

# 27

# Only One Thing

*Martha was distracted by the big dinner she was preparing. She came to Jesus and said, "Lord, doesn't it seem unfair to you that my sister just sits here while I do all the work? Tell her to come and help me." But the Lord said to her, "My dear Martha, you are worried and upset over all these details! There is only one thing worth being concerned about. Mary has discovered it, and it will not be taken away from her."* Luke 10:40-42

Boy, does this sound familiar. Ugh! I have muttered a variation of Martha's words when I've been preparing a big dinner. I did not say them directly to Jesus, but I might as well have been talking to Him. Like Martha, I get worried and upset over a lot of details too!

Let's be honest. What woman hasn't had "Martha moments" from time to time, when she feels she has taken on more than she can manage?

Jesus responds quickly: "My dear Martha, my dear Kim, my dear sweet you, you are worried and upset over all these details! There is only one thing worth being concerned about. Mary has discovered it, and it will not be taken away from her."

Only one thing is needed, and that is connecting with the Lord Himself. Sweet Martha was distracted in the details, while Sweet Mary got the "only one thing" right: focusing on Jesus. As the old hymn says, we need to "turn our eyes upon Jesus, look full in His wonderful face, and the things of earth will grow strangely dim in the light of His glory and grace."

When we pause to focus on Jesus first, He either eases our stressed-out spirits or changes our attitudes in the circumstances that threaten to undo us. He wants us to pause in His presence and be mindful of who He is and the amazing things He has done for us. I know that sounds counterproductive, even a misuse of time when we are in a tizzy. Truthfully, He is just what we need to adjust our priorities and to be able to encourage others around us.

• • • • • • • • • •

LET'S BE CONCERNED ABOUT ONE THING—THE LORD!
CLEAR A SPACE ON YOUR REFRIGERATOR AND STICK
A NOTE UP THERE THAT SAYS, "ONE THING!"

## Be Encouraged!

*This is my command—be strong and courageous!*
*Do not be afraid or discouraged. For the LORD your*
*God is with you wherever you go.* Joshua 1:9

God doesn't want us to be discouraged, but sometimes it happens. On those mornings when I wake up feeling discouraged, I ask Him to encourage me and to give me courage for that day. I know that my Father always knows best and He wants to lift my heavy heart.

*Encourage* simply means "to give courage to." God gives courage to my heart when I open His Word and hear Him speak. For the longest time I thought He spoke only to the important people in church—the pastors, the evangelists, the Sunday school teachers, and the Bible study leaders. I did not know that our *big God* would talk to *little me* straight from His Word. When I began going to Him every morning with my Bible in hand, I started to hear His voice resonate in my heart and soul.

Spending time in God's Word is no longer just a morning check-off on my to-do list. It is a way of life. I do not want to miss anything He has to say to me. If I take time to reflect on His words, an interesting thing happens—those words follow me around throughout the day. I find if I get dressed and get my shoes on before I meet with Him, I am out the door. But when I let the dishes soak a little longer and keep my bedroom slippers on, it forces me to slow down and park myself in His Word. He gives me courage by His Spirit, encouragement that will overflow to others. He is the best Encourager there is.

• • • • • • • • • • •

LET'S PARK OURSELVES IN HIS PRESENCE AS MUCH AS WE CAN. EVEN IN THE MIDST OF OUR LONG TO-DO LISTS, WE NEED TO LISTEN TO GOD AND BE ENCOURAGED!

# 29

# Whatever!

*And whatever you do, whether in word or deed, do it all in the name of the Lord Jesus, giving thanks to God the Father through him.* Colossians 3:17, NIV (emphasis mine)

This verse gives new meaning to the word *whatever* that is often used as an exasperated response from a teenager's lips! The apostle Paul isn't using the word here with a begrudging tone. Instead, this *whatever* embraces all the potential joy it can pass on. Whatever you and I do as God's children, we can do with a thankful heart in Jesus' name. It brings to my mind the song that the seven dwarfs sang in *Snow White*, "Whistle While You Work." (Wouldn't that make Walt Disney proud?)

A believer's every action points to Christ! Lest those actions reflect negatively on our Savior, Paul encourages us to remember that we have countless opportunities each day to uphold Christ's name. *Whatever* we do or say in Jesus' name, giving thanks, happens only through His Spirit living in us.

The book of Colossians was written to believers in the church in Colosse, people who had already put their faith and trust in Christ. But some of those believers were thinking their salvation depended on "doing the commandments." Paul was reminding all of them (and us) that Christ alone is sufficient, and His sufficiency makes it possible to get our eyes off of ourselves and our human goals, and focus on Jesus. Reflecting Him will draw others to want to know Him too.

Colossians begins with C, as in "Christ first." As believers in Christ, we need to heed Paul's reminder, too, and not confuse the truth of today's verse as a way to earn merit with God. When we focus on Him, we grow to love Him more. As we love Him more, our *whatevers* become opportunities to experience and express His joy as we represent Him in this world, which is so quickly moving toward isolation.

* * * * * * * * * *

AS WE GO THROUGH THE DAY, LET'S BE MINDFUL OF
*WHATEVER* WAYS WE CAN REPRESENT HIM WELL IN
A WORLD THAT NEEDS TO KNOW THE REAL JESUS.

# 30

# Becoming a Better Listener

*Spouting off before listening to the facts is both
shameful and foolish.* Proverbs 18:13

I have been keeping a list of Bible verses that mention
our mouths because, frankly, sometimes my mouth
needs to be buttoned up.

At times I am as impulsive as the disciple Peter, who
got so excited that he practically jumped out of a boat
to walk on the water to Jesus, only to begin to falter and
sink when he let his attention be diverted from the Lord.

Yes, my impulsiveness is often expressed verbally. I
may interrupt someone out of excitement or fear that I
am going to forget something important if I don't blurt
it out immediately. In fact, my early-morning phone
friend, Daphne, and I are working on not interrupting
each other, but it's hard because we have a lot to cover in
such a short amount of time!

Being talkative isn't a bad thing, but the more
talkative we are, the more we open ourselves up to
can't-take-back words flowing from our lips. Our family
friend Skip used to say he did not enjoy being around
BMWs (Big-Mouth Women). Abrupt, intrusive talk is
not becoming to a godly woman *or* man.

"Lord, how many times have I answered a family member or a coworker or a friend without listening?"

When others speak, I want to listen because I really do care about them. Today's verse reminds me to pause before letting every thought become verbal. The book of Proverbs is practical because it reveals so many of our weaknesses and our sin, but in such a positive way. Solomon tells us how to reflect more of Christ through these wise sayings.

God is the only perfect talker and listener. He hears everything, and He is always available. He never does or says anything wrong. He does not react impulsively, but instead responds thoughtfully for our good, even though the truth is sometimes difficult for us to hear. Because He wants us to reflect His gracious truth more fully, if we need help in this area, we only need to ask and listen.

. . . . . . . . . . .

TODAY LET'S BE WISE WOMEN WHO LISTEN FOR HIS WISDOM. LET'S WORK ON REALLY LISTENING TO PEOPLE WITHOUT INTERRUPTING OR THINKING OF THE CLEVER COMEBACKS WE HAVE READY.

# 31

# I'm In!

*Jesus said to the people who believed in him, "You are truly my disciples if you remain faithful to my teachings. And you will know the truth, and the truth will set you free."* John 8:31-32

*I*m in, Lord, I'm in, I'm in! I believe You are talking to me. I want to remain faithful to Your teaching and, more importantly, faithful to You!

No half-pint living for me! I want to be a gallon jug of sweet tea, filled to overflowing, that is fresh every day and perpetually full so it can be continually poured out to others. I would call that kind of living about as abundant as it can be!

To experience this abundance requires that we grow to be faithful, but what does being faithful look like? *Faithful* is an adjective, a part of speech that describes another word. A faithful person is one who is reliable, dependable, firm, sure, unswerving, conscientious, and steadfast—all qualities that describe Jesus. I love being around God's faithful people, don't you? They look like Christ, and He is beautifully apparent in those who are faithfully His.

Living in complete faithfulness is a choice. Choosing God's way over our own requires multiple decisions every day, but they are the best decisions you and I can make!

The Holy Spirit inside of us is the One who gives us this desire to remain completely faithful. The only way you and I can stay true to Christ is to stay attached to Him, our faithful Vine, as He pours Himself into us. He is 100 percent reliable, dependable, firm, sure, unswerving, conscientious, and steadfast. When we let Him have His way in us, we will grow in faithfulness.

. . . . . . . . . . .

CONSIDER FOR A FEW MOMENTS WHAT YOUR LIFE— AND THIS WHOLE WORLD, FOR THAT MATTER—WOULD BE LIKE IF GOD WERE LESS THAN 100 PERCENT FAITHFUL. THANK HIM THAT BECAUSE HE IS ALL IN, THROUGH HIM WE CAN BE ALL IN TOO!

32

# What Diet Are You On?

*I have rejoiced in your laws as much as in riches.
I will study your commandments and reflect on
your ways. I will delight in your decrees and
not forget your word.* Psalm 119:14-16

I used to wonder why my mama would ask my younger sister, Shawn, so many questions when we were growing up because she didn't seem to ask me very many. I felt like I was put on a "no question diet," and I did not like it! Years later, I finally asked Mama, and she told me that I always told her everything, while my sister needed prompting!

God made us all different, didn't He? The Bible is where God tells us everything He wants us to know. He does not have us on a "no question diet." He wants us to know about Him. He reveals His never-ending love, grace, justice, and mercy over and over in Psalm 119, the longest psalm in the Bible and one of my all-time favorites! In 176 verses, it lists the benefits of God's Word. For starters, God's Word

- revives us (verse 25)
- encourages us (verse 28)

- expands our understanding (verse 32)
- gives us an eagerness for His laws (verse 36)
- reassures us of His promises (verse 38)
- helps us abandon our shameful ways (verse 39)
- renews our life with His goodness (verse 40).

God tells us what He is like, what we are like, and how much we need Him. His Word is a nourishing feast for our souls and healing balm to our hurts and vulnerabilities. Reading His Word increases our appetite for living His way. It is one diet that we can never over-indulge on.

. . . . . . . . . . .

WE NEVER NEED TO DIET WHEN IT COMES TO GOD'S WORD! IT SHOWS US WHAT HE IS LIKE, WHAT WE ARE LIKE, AND HOW MUCH WE NEED HIM. INDULGE IN PSALM 119 TODAY.

# 33

## God Never Exaggerates

*I am with you always, even to the end of the age.*
Matthew 28:20

We don't always mean to do it, but it happens: We tend to exaggerate. Have you ever caught yourself saying, "I'm starving"? How about "I'm dead on my feet"? Maybe someone has accused you of *never* doing something or *always* doing something else. These are pretty big statements to make.

According to Webster's dictionary, the word *exaggerate* means to overstate, or think or tell of something as greater than it is. Haven't we been taught that words like *always* and *never* hinder our communication with others, that many times using them fuels confrontations? I'm so encouraged by the fact that God never exaggerates.

All through Scripture, God communicates His unexaggerated but extravagant love for us through His Son, Jesus Christ, whom He sent to die on the cross for our sins. What loving earthly father would give the life of his only son or daughter for the life of another person? God did that for all of mankind. God gave His Son for you. God gave His Son for me!

The Word of God is full of claims that may seem like boasts or exaggerations, but they are really true statements.

To *all* who did receive him, to those who believed in his name, he gave the right to become children of God. John 1:12, NIV

God is the King of *all* the earth. Psalm 47:7, NIV

[Love] *always* protects, *always* trusts, *always* hopes, *always* perseveres.
I CORINTHIANS 13:7, NIV

He will *never* leave you nor forsake you. Deuteronomy 31:6, NIV (emphasis added in all of the verses quoted)

God is the only One who can say these words honestly every single time.

. . . . . . . . . .

EVERY TIME YOU READ THESE WORDS IN SCRIPTURE—
ALL, ALWAYS, OR *NEVER*—HIGHLIGHT THEM IN YOUR
BIBLE. AND REMEMBER, GOD NEVER EXAGGERATES!

# 34

## Hiding the Sweets

*Turn my eyes from worthless things, and give
me life through your word.* Psalm 119:37

**M**y husband enjoys going to the grocery store, but it
is not on my list of favorite things to do, although I do
love to eat the goodies we buy from there. And sometimes the treats are big temptations.

I teasingly call Mark "My Snack Man." When he
goes to the grocery store, he stocks up on the sweet and
salty snacks we both love. I recently asked him to hide
them from me in a place where I could not readily see
them. He has more self-control than I do. We don't nag
each other about dieting at all, but since I am trying
to eat healthier, I don't want the sweets staring me in
the face.

I've never been tempted by lima beans, chicken
livers, or any piece of meat that is an appendage. But put
a cookie near me, and a little voice inside of me says that
if I eat them all, there won't be any left to be tempted by.
I confess that, in a weak moment, I have succumbed to
eating half a pack of Girl Scout Thin Mint cookies.

To try to avoid junk food, I tell myself that sweets
are worthless to me. Of course, cookies are not totally
worthless, but when I mentally place them in that

category, it helps me maintain my focus on what's best for me to eat. My lack of self-control makes it clear that I need God's guidance in all parts of my life.

In the context of this psalm, the worthless things could be anything that distracts us from the Lord and His Word.

Through His Word, God not only instructs me but motivates me by His Spirit to make better choices in all things, not just food, and to minimize the distractions. We all struggle and are tempted by "worthless things." God knows our weaknesses and tendency to depend on things for comfort and satisfaction. He will guide us by His Spirit to implement changes in areas of our lives when we submit ourselves to Him.

* * * * * * * * * *

LET'S NOT BE AFRAID TO ASK OUR FAMILY
AND FRIENDS FOR HELP, TOO, IN TURNING
OUR EYES FROM "WORTHLESS THINGS."

# Come Boldly

*Since we have a great High Priest who has entered heaven,
Jesus the Son of God, let us hold firmly to what we believe.
. . . So let us come boldly to the throne of our gracious
God. There we will receive his mercy, and we will find
grace to help us when we need it most.* Hebrews 4:14, 16

When I was in college preparing to be a teacher, I
was fascinated by different learning styles. The way our
brains process information and how we communicate
is very complex. I am someone who processes information verbally, which explains why I tend to leave long
phone messages.

Yes, I am an out-loud processor who sometimes gets
overly excited and says too much. It can be embarrass-
ing. Most men do not like hearing all the details, so I
am horrified if I leave a fun message for a friend whose
husband happens to hear it. Unlike me, Mark processes
and summarizes information internally. He figures out
what he is going to say before he says a word, while
I think out loud.

When I read today's verses from Hebrews, I was so
relieved. God clearly wants us to come boldly to Him,
whether we blurt out all our thoughts or present them
logically. He does not care how we express them. He

70

simply wants us to come to Him. It is better to get things out with God than to hold back, because He knows our hearts either way. Not only is it cleansing to confess, rant, and rave to Him about someone hurting you or decisions you must make, but talking with God first can prevent us from gossiping about an issue with a friend. Spending time with Him gives Him the opportunity to work on our hearts and show us if our feelings and rantings are misguided, and He sends His calming Spirit to settle us.

God will always have the right response to us. He wants us to come to Him as we are, no matter what our communication style may be. How freeing is that!

* * * * * * * * *

BECAUSE OF CHRIST AND OUR FAITH IN HIM, WE CAN COME BOLDLY AND CONFIDENTLY INTO GOD'S PRESENCE. WRITE DOWN EPHESIANS 3:12 AS A REMINDER TO SHARE WITH HIM WHATEVER IS ON YOUR HEART TODAY.

# *Fighting Your Battles*

*This is the LORD's battle, and he will give you to us!*
1 Samuel 17:47

I envy David's confidence portrayed in this verse. He was facing a giant named Goliath, ready to fight him to the death with a few stones flung from a slingshot and plenty of big faith. David was able to fight confidently because he knew who was ultimately going to win his battle—the Lord! It wasn't little "d" fighting big "g." It was big G—God—fighting "little" Goliath.

Like me, you are probably fighting some personal battles. We can fight with faith, too, because our battles also belong to the Lord!

Faith assures us that Christ is beside us. He knows every detail about all the circumstances we're up against. Even in the darkest moments, our comrade, Jesus Christ, is with us. He knows His victory is sure, and He guards us with His life. He camouflages us from being an unguarded target for the enemy. This knowledge about our great Warrior is our confidence to keep moving forward in life's battles.

When I was unexpectedly diagnosed with breast cancer in 2004, everything in my life seemed to change so quickly. During my mastectomy when I was under anesthesia, I was literally in the dark, hoping for a reconstructed breast when I woke up. When I awakened, I learned that both surgeons had made a judgment call and delayed reconstruction so my chemotherapy and radiation treatments would not be slowed down. When I saw myself in the mirror for the first time, I said to my husband, Mark, "Now I know why they call cancer a battle." I felt how a wounded soldier must feel when he or she is sent home from war.

But then God helped me see something: My battle with cancer was really His battle, not mine. I belonged to Him, and He would fight for me. God was doing an important reconstruction on my heart then, and thankfully, He continues to reconstruct me inside and out to this day.

We all know the feeling of being in the dark, unable to see something but believing it is there. Moving forward in the dark certainly requires faith. This faith fuels our hope when we faithful believers in Christ are in dark, painful places. We always need faith. We always need God.

. . . . . . . . . .

THE BATTLE IS NOT OURS BUT THE LORD'S!
READ 1 TIMOTHY 6:12 TO GET YOUR
ONGOING MARCHING ORDERS.

## *Lifelong Resolution*

*May God give you more and more grace
and peace as you grow in your knowledge of
God and Jesus our Lord.* 2 Peter 1:2

More and more grace and peace! More and more growth in my knowledge of God and Jesus my Lord. Doesn't that sound wonderful? Don't we all long for more grace and peace in our personal lives, in our families, in our world?

Sometimes it is difficult to describe the deep meaning of those words, but I sure know when I am *not* experiencing God's peace. "His peace will guard your hearts and minds as you live in Christ Jesus" (Philippians 4:7).

His peace is a gift we can share with others, something that I don't always do consistently. The same is true for God's grace. I sure know when I am not extending God's grace to people, although I usually discover it after the fact. I am stingiest with grace when I am on the phone with a technician on the other side of the globe who is remotely troubleshooting a problem with my computer, television, or phone. I am ashamed to say I have had to call a technician back and humbly apologize for my irritation and curt responses. My forever resolution each day of each year is to know Jesus more and more—to open my heart to receive His grace and peace, be renewed, and never miss anything He has for me!

How do we get to know God? After receiving Christ by faith, we become part of His family. As we read the Bible, we experience Him more personally, especially understanding how He deals with His people and what we need to do to live for Him. Why would any of us want to miss out on anything God Almighty has planned?

• • • • • • • • • •

KNOW JESUS AND GROW! DISCOVER HOW KNOWING JESUS AND STAYING CLOSE TO HIM AFFECTS EVERY AREA OF YOUR LIFE BY READING JOHN 15:1–17.

# 38

# There's a Whole Lotta Shakin' Goin' On

*I know the LORD is always with me. I will not be shaken, for he is right beside me.* Psalm 16:8

It sounds funny now, but this fifties song by Jerry Lee Lewis actually came to mind when a 5.8-magnitude earthquake hit my neck of the woods. Measurable earthquakes are rare in Virginia. The tremors struck without warning. I didn't have time to run for the bathtub, so I just shook and waited.

Although the unsettled floor beneath my feet felt strange, I didn't panic. My spirit remained calm, thanks to the Holy Spirit's power. I was not really alone. I know the Bible's promise in today's verse—that the Lord was right beside me. Repeatedly in His Word, He says that He will be ever present with His children.

It seems that every day there is some natural disaster happening somewhere in our world. Sometimes I catch myself wondering what I would do if I were caught in the midst of a devastating, seemingly hopeless catastrophe. Then I remember that God will be present in those crises, too, and my fears subside. We cannot get away from His presence; we cannot escape His watchful care over us. Because I belong to God, if the earth swallowed me one moment, I would be looking directly at the face of God the next.

Today's verse comes from what I call Psalm Sweet 16. No matter how much shaking is going on in our lives—financially, emotionally, physically, spiritually—we can confidently trust God. The Lord wants us not only to survive whatever we're going through but to truly thrive in His abundant presence even more deeply during shaky times.

He is our solid Rock who will keep us grounded now and forever. I like that it says in Psalm 18:36 from *The Message*: "You cleared the ground under me so my footing was firm."

. . . . . . . . . .

READ PSALM 16:11 OUT LOUD, CONFIDENTLY REPEATING DAVID'S WORDS: "YOU WILL SHOW ME THE WAY OF LIFE, GRANTING ME THE JOY OF YOUR PRESENCE AND THE PLEASURES OF LIVING WITH YOU FOREVER."

# 39

# I Live You

*Those who obey God's word truly show how completely they love him. That is how we know we are living in him. Those who say they live in God should live their lives as Jesus did.* 1 John 2:5-6

It happens repeatedly to me when I'm texting on my phone's teeny keyboard. I hit the *i* key instead of the *o* key and sign off my messages with "I *live* you" instead of "I *love* you."

I've thought about my unintentional misspelling in terms of my relationship with God. We *love* Him when we *live* Him. We *live* Him when we *obey* Him. And when we *obey* Him, we *love* and *live* Him. That's all there is to it! The best part is that when we have given our lives to Christ, His Spirit inside us gives us the "want to." We want to do His will. "God is working in you, giving you the desire and the power to do what pleases him" (Philippians 2:13). Isn't this wonderful news? We want to please Him, and even that desire comes from Him! God is always at work in His children's lives.

It makes sense. If you're like me, you want to show your family and close friends how much you love them. We want to please them, so we do things that we know they like. Here's a simple example: I try to remember to clean off my clutter from our small bathroom counter so my husband, Mark, has room for his things. All of us have choices, and when we choose to take God's high road in the big and small things, we live Him over and over again. What a wonderful, freeing way to live!

. . . . . . . . . .

WHAT SMALL CHANGE DO YOU NEED TO MAKE TO
LIVE GOD BEFORE A FAMILY MEMBER OR FRIEND?
TRY TO IMPLEMENT IT QUICKLY AND LIVE HIM.

# 40

# Clinging to Him

*I cling to you; your strong right hand holds me securely.*
Psalm 63:8

I have already confessed that I suffer from an incurable habit of space invasion in my devotion "Confessions of a Leaner." I have always liked to sit close to people—shoulder-to-shoulder, elbow-to-elbow. Even when walking down the street while shopping with my daughter or girl-friends, I tend to move into their personal space without realizing that I am sometimes too close for their comfort! But thankfully, we always end up laughing about this habit of mine!

Isn't it wonderful that God wants us to sit close to Him? We can never get too close for His comfort. Not only does He want us to stay close whether we're sitting or walking or running through life together, but He tells us to cling to Him—to tailgate, hang on, piggyback, however you want to express it—to never let go, *ever*! He does not want us to drop His hand.

I love to visualize sticking so close to Him that no one can squeeze between us—because *we are tight*! What an absolutely fabulous ride to live life clinging to a strong and loving Father who never shrugs us off or nudges us out of His way. I long to cling to Him so I will not skip off the path or take a detour; I don't want to miss a stop on His personal journey for me, not even for a second. His way is the best way. He is always in the lead, and He ensures that the stops He makes are only for my good. Even if the stop does not appear inviting to me, He is still there, helping me see that He will bring good from the experience. Clinging to Him, I will never be lost or alone.

If you are unsure whether you are connected to God, He is ready and willing to take your hand and pull you close. It's your move to put yourself in His big hand every day and never let go.

• • • • • • • • • •

LET'S CLING TO CHRIST! WE CAN START BY MAKING JAMES 4:8 (NIV) OUR VERSE TODAY: "COME NEAR TO GOD AND HE WILL COME NEAR TO YOU."

# 41

# Picking Priorities

*Seek the Kingdom of God above all else,*
*and live righteously.* Matthew 6:33

How in the world do I wisely arrange my days, hours, and minutes—coordinating schedules and responsibilities—and still find time to rest? There's much to accomplish. As I find myself daily being attentive to both my family's needs and my work schedule, I must stop and ask myself whether my days are reflecting my priorities.

Years ago when I was a student, my ears perked up during a sermon in church when the pastor said, "There are only three things that are going to last in this world: God, His Word, and people."

Right then I decided my life's priorities. Little did that pastor know how much God would use him to help me make daily decisions and choices for the rest of my life. Why would I want to invest my time in anything that doesn't matter? His words come back to me frequently and prompt me to consider my everyday priorities:

- Am I seeking the things of God above all else?
- Why would I want to invest my time and resources in anything that isn't going to last?

- Are the things that are important to God important to me, no matter what my occupation, and do I work with God's eternal mind-set?
- Do I crave God's Word, knowing it truly is sweeter than anything else?
- Do I live as salt among the people in my life, looking for ways God can use me to help create a thirst for Him in them?

This list helps me apply that pastor's wisdom from the Bible to keep God, His Word, and people as top priorities. When we filter our schedules through this checklist of the heart, we can adjust our time according to God's priorities for us.

* * * * * * * * * * *

## PICK ETERNAL PRIORITIES WITH SIMPLE, SWEET, AND SALTY LIVES FOR JESUS CHRIST.

# 42

## *Falling in Love*

*The LORD helps the fallen and lifts those
bent beneath their loads.* Psalm 145:14

It hurts to fall. Most of the time, falling hurts on the inside even if it doesn't really hurt on the outside. I have had my share of falls. I've tripped over my tall husband's basketball player–sized feet, and I have fallen in a hole or two or three. In each instance, my pride feels wounded every bit as much as my bruised muscles or scraped skin.

If I had a choice, I would choose physical pain over emotional pain. I have an extremely high pain threshold, so I'm able to deal with physical pain pretty well. But emotional pain is another story. It can cause excruciating pain that no anti-inflammatory medicine can touch. No matter what the origin of our emotional pain or the level of our pain threshold, our hearts need healing!

You may be hurting from emotional pain today. Maybe you are struggling to put one foot in front of the other. Possibly the circumstances in your life have changed drastically overnight and you feel battered to the point that you can't even seem to stand on your own.

I'm so thankful that there is one type of fall that feels wonderful! Falling in love can't be beat, especially when it comes to falling in love with the Lord. I have definitely fallen in love with Him through His Word. If my heart is heavy and I feel bent beneath my load, I run to the Lord in the Psalms. There I am reminded of His strong help and kind care.

Jesus lifts up all those who are burdened with heartache. As we look to the Lord in hope, we can trust that the Great Physician's timing is always best. When we fall down—and we all do—the Lord Almighty is upholding us and will lift us up in His way and time.

. . . . . . . . . .

READ ALL OF PSALM 145. PRAISE HIM FOR ALL HIS "AWE-INSPIRING DEEDS" (VERSE 6) OF LOVE THAT HAVE ALREADY TAKEN PLACE IN YOUR LIFE AS WELL AS THOSE YET TO COME.

# 43

# The Power of His Word

*The word of God is alive and powerful. It is sharper
than the sharpest two-edged sword, cutting between
soul and spirit, between joint and marrow. It
exposes our innermost thoughts and desires. Nothing
in all creation is hidden from God. Everything is
naked and exposed before his eyes, and he is the one
to whom we are accountable.* Hebrews 4:12-13

One of my God-given roles as a wife is to be my husband's helper. While I heartily embrace this, there are
times when I don't find it easy to live up to that role,
especially when it requires me to do something I don't
feel like doing.

Recently Mark asked me to help him by making a
phone call early in the morning. I was reluctant to do
it because I was in the middle of my Bible study and
I knew it would mean spending a lot of time waiting
through endless prompts. (I'm sure the day's study had
to do with putting others' needs above our own.)

As I sat there, the Holy Spirit nudged my reluctant heart and cut through my bad attitude while I
was reading God's Word. Here are a few thoughts He
brought to my mind:

*Where did that selfish, sinful attitude come from?*
    (Answer: Mark 7:21-23)
*I forget so quickly there is a war going on in my soul!*
    (Galatians 5:17)
*But Lord, I want to be like You.* (Colossians 3:12-13)

God's Word shows me what I am really like, and I am eternally grateful for that. Talk about "cutting between soul and spirit, between joint and marrow"! It sounds like an amputation, and it feels like one, too, when our "innermost thoughts and desires" are exposed! No wonder I hurt when I sin against God. The best part of this problem? Jesus! He died on the cross and paid the price for all of our sins forever.

"Lord, thank You that I am not alone and completely undone in this struggle. Even Paul, your faithful servant, struggled with sin, but he also reminded us of our Rescuer!"

. . . . . . . . . .

THANK GOD FOR HIS VITAL AND POWERFUL WORD! READ ABOUT THE APOSTLE PAUL'S STRUGGLE WITH SIN IN ROMANS 7:21–8:2.

# 44

# Piles to Go before I Sleep

*For everything there is a season, a time for every
activity under heaven. . . . A time to keep and
a time to throw away.* Ecclesiastes 3:1, 6

At some point in my education I had to memorize
Robert Frost's famous poem "Stopping by Woods on a
Snowy Evening." I like the images that the poet created,
but to be honest, that's not my life. Forgive me, Mr.
Frost. I've changed the last two lines of your poem from
"*miles* to go before I sleep" to "*piles* to go before I sleep,
and *piles* to go before I sleep." That's a more accurate
description of what I face each day.

Can you relate? Many of us have big and small piles
around us, whether they're on the desk, in the sink,
or by the bed—piles of papers, piles of dishes, or piles
of reading materials. If you are a crafts person, you
might have piles of projects, piles of photos, or piles
of fabric. If you are into the latest beauty products, you
might have accumulated piles of lipstick (that really
won't come off when you eat!) or piles of "age defying"
makeup.

There is nothing wrong with material things. There
is a time to keep things and a time to throw them away

(Ecclesiastes 3:6). Anything around us that distracts us from God's specific plan for our lives is clutter and needs to be discarded. I think it is that simple. Your clutter might not look like my clutter, but that's okay. We need to stop comparing piles and allow God to help us clean up our own. This frees us for simple priority living—investing our time in God, His Word, and people.

• • • • • • • • • •

IDENTIFY ONE PHYSICAL AND ONE SPIRITUAL PILE TODAY THAT WEIGHS YOU DOWN. THEN TAKE ACTION. MAYBE IT'S TIME TO DROP OFF A DONATION AT THE LOCAL RESALE SHOP. AND IF YOU HAVE LOST YOUR TEMPER WITH SOMEONE, ASK FOR FORGIVENESS.

# 45

# Where Are You Headed?

*You are citizens along with all of God's holy people.*
*You are members of God's family.* Ephesians 2:19

I have a confession to make: I really don't enjoy exercising this side of heaven.

It's not that I mind the actual physical exertion part. The problem is that I only like to get ready once per day! The thought of driving somewhere in workout wear, exercising, *then* showering and changing into regular clothes seems like too much of a rigmarole to me. Plus, if I were in a class with others I hadn't seen in a while, I'd want to know what God was doing in their lives, and I'd be more interested in reaching out to them than getting my heart rate up.

But guess what? I know that the Lord wants us to be good stewards of the bodies He has given us, and in midlife, by God's grace, I've discovered that I am motivated to walk several miles if I have a destination. When a new sidewalk was put in near my neighborhood, I discovered that it conveniently led to the coffee shop a mile and a half away. I *sometimes* enjoy the three-mile round-trip trek for coffee and a quiet bench with my teeny Bible—the perfect size for a hand weight. Hallelujah!

I think I may have found an exercise plan that works for me. It was all about the destination.

More crucial than a geographical destination is our eternal destination. When we die, we are all headed somewhere, whether we believe it or not. If we believe in Christ, we are already citizens of heaven while journeying here on earth. We are being made ready for our heavenly home through trusting in Him.

• • • • • • • • • • •

ARE YOU EXERCISING YOUR HEAVENLY CITIZENSHIP
WHILE HERE ON EARTH? REMIND YOURSELF OF
YOUR TRUE HOME WITH JESUS AND LIVE YOUR LIFE
RIGHT NOW AS IF YOU'RE HOMEWARD BOUND.

# 46

# Hope

*Why am I discouraged? (Why am I discouraged?) Why is
my heart so sad? (Why is my heart so sad?) I will put my
hope in God! (I will put my hope in God!) I will praise
him again—my Savior and my God! (I will praise him
again—my Savior and my God!)* Psalm 42:11 (Psalm 43:5)

It's okay. You don't need to get your eyes checked after
reading today's verses. It's really not an error. Both of
these psalms end with the same chorus. In fact, in many
Hebrew manuscripts these two psalms are combined as
a single song.

Are you discouraged today? Did you wake up with
a "so sad" heart? I mentioned to Mark that I have
been writing some of these devotions during one of
the saddest times in my life, after I lost my precious
mother to cancer. Mama taught me everything I know
about creating a warm and welcoming home. Do you
know what Mark said? "A lot of the psalms were written
during sad, difficult times too." He's right. It must be
why I relish reading a psalm every day! God gets me! I'm
not alone! He understands how heavy my heart is.

These two psalms (along with Psalms 44–49) are
attributed to the descendants of Korah, a choir of
temple singers who had been appointed by King David.

Here they may be lamenting a time when they were in exile. Discouragement and sadness are universal problems, even for men and women of faith. But then comes the answer to the cries of lament: "I will put my hope in God!"

I remember being just out of college, visiting a church in Tennessee where I heard a pastor use this acrostic for hope:

Happy
Optimism of
Promises
Expected!

Whenever I am struggling with sadness that seems to sap all my energy or discouragement that is difficult even to express at times, I will focus on God. When I dwell on His Word, praise just naturally follows—and so does HOPE . . . Happy Optimism of Promises Expected!

* * * * * * * * * *

## CHOOSE HOPE IN CHRIST. READ ROMANS 15:13.

# 47

# Glorious New Clothes

*We know that if the earthly tent we live in is destroyed,*
*we have a building from God, an eternal house in*
*heaven, not built by human hands. Meanwhile we*
*groan, longing to be clothed instead with our heavenly*
*dwelling, because when we are clothed, we will*
*not be found naked.* 2 Corinthians 5:1-3, NIV

Every day I feel like a brand-new mother. Every stage is new when you only have one child and have not passed this way before. Sometimes I can be too conscientious for my own good or for my family's. I want to do it right, but many times I am not sure just what to do or say in certain circumstances. One thing I have learned over the years is that the truth is always a great place to start.

When our daughter was five, we had to go to our first family funeral. As an inexperienced mother, I was anxious about how to prepare her for the receiving line, the casket, the tears, and the grave. I told her the truth: We would see her great-grandmother in a casket, but it was her body, a shell. Her spirit was in heaven with Jesus, and she would never cry again or have pain. We would see her again when we go to heaven!

Like any curious five-year-old, Kali wanted to touch

her great-grandmother when we went for the visitation. Later, on the way home, she said, "Mommy, why did Grandmommy Newlen have her clothes on?"

I was so afraid I had ruined her for life by taking her, and I wanted to pass over her question quickly. I simply said, "She just needed to be modest," knowing full well that Kali did not know what the word *modest* meant.

The next day, out of sheer curiosity, I asked her why she had asked me that question. She said, "Because Mommy, when you go to heaven you get new clothes, and she needs to be 'nekkid' to get them on. I can't wait to see Grandmommy Newlen in her glorious new clothes!" *Glorious?* What a wonderful surprise word to hear from the mouth of a babe. I'm *sure* it brought glory to God.

Casket closed!

* * * * * * * * * *

# HAVE SOME FUN TODAY IMAGINING WHAT YOUR HEAVENLY CLOTHING WILL LOOK LIKE. IT WILL BE GLORIOUS!

# 48

# First Find Out . . .

*Jehoshaphat added, "But first let's find out what the LORD says."* 1 Kings 22:5

Jehoshaphat had a good idea. When I read these true accounts of kings and battles, of victories and defeats throughout God's Word, I feel like putting on my pink army boots. I am reminded that even though I don't have a chariot and a sword, I am fighting some personal battles, just as you probably are. It doesn't matter if the battles are big or small; they all require us to make decisions.

This fascinating chapter begins with a three-year blessing of peace between the nation of Israel and its neighbors. During this time Jehoshaphat, the king of Judah, visited King Ahab of Israel. Ahab was readying plans to lay siege to Ramoth-gilead, which he believed rightfully belonged to Israel. Ahab asked Jehoshaphat if he would go into battle with him against the king of Aram.

As I read it, I started thinking, *Good idea.* "Two people are better off than one, for they can help each other succeed" (Ecclesiastes 4:9). But then I cheered for Jehoshaphat because I *loved* his reply to Ahab: "First let's find out what the LORD says." Jehoshaphat had a much better idea than Ahab!

When you and I have decisions to make, it's important for us to first find out what God says. We need to lay our own hearts and plans on the table, more for our benefit than God's, because He already knows we need help and He sees what is on the other side of our decision. Actually He sees all sides of the decision.

We need to be sure we are listening to His wise commands in Scripture. God will never go against His Word or tell us to do something contrary to it. With the Holy Spirit's power, we are never alone in battle. Our assignment is to surrender to His strategy and obey whatever practical steps He shows us, realizing that the fight is under His control. When we listen to His battle plan, we can be confident that the victory is not on our shoulders—it's on His, and He always wins!

. . . . . . . . . .

WHEN YOU NEED TO MAKE A DECISION, FIRST FIND OUT WHAT THE LORD SAYS! REVIEW EPHESIANS 6:10-17 TO BECOME FAMILIAR WITH HOW GOD EQUIPS YOU FOR ALL THE BIG AND SMALL SKIRMISHES IN LIFE.

# 49

## "So Excited" Face

*Don't rejoice because evil spirits obey you; rejoice because
your names are registered in heaven.* Luke 10:20

Sometimes I get so excited about what God does that
I just cannot seem to keep it in. My sweet friend Alison
calls it my "so excited" face.

In Luke 10, Jesus sent out seventy-two of His followers ahead of Him to all the towns and places He
planned to visit. In Luke 10:17 when they returned to
report back to Jesus, it's not hard to imagine that they
had on their "so excited" faces, too, because they eagerly
told Him, "Lord, even the demons obey us when we use
your name!"

But it is Jesus' response to His followers that really
intrigues me. They were reveling in the successful ministry God had given them, a mission that had seen results.
Jesus reminded His followers of the good things He had
given them, like the authority to trample on snakes and
scorpions and to overcome the power of the enemy so
nothing would harm them. But then He said something
unexpected: "But don't rejoice because evil spirits obey
you; rejoice because your names are registered in heaven"
(Luke 10:20).

This word *don't* gives us perspective when we have

on our "so excited" faces for what God has done in our lives, our work, and our families. When we have experienced His power and cannot keep it in, we glory in Him and our position in Him for all eternity. Even when it seems that our mission has failed, we can truly be joyful because in Christ, our names are written in heaven—signed, sealed, and delivered by His sacrifice for you and me! Now that's something to have a "so excited" face about!

. . . . . . . . . .

IF WE ARE NOT WEARING OUR "SO EXCITED"
FACES, LET'S THINK OF WHAT JESUS DID FOR US.
THEN WRITE A THANK-YOU NOTE TO HIM.

# 50

# Sweet Rest

*He lets me rest in green meadows; he leads me beside
peaceful streams. He renews my strength.* Psalm 23:2-3

I don't know about you, but sometimes I feel as though
a stressed-out state is the norm. Feeling rested and
peaceful seems to be a rarity for our culture. Many of
us experience sleep deprivation, but when we add the
stresses and troubles of everyday life or full-fledged
suffering, we've got the recipe for physical, emotional,
mental, spiritual, and relational exhaustion.

I'm guessing you can relate. Just because we live in
an age where things have become easier for us doesn't
mean we won't feel worn out. Glance at Psalms and
you'll see that weariness has always had the power to
catch up with anyone, no matter when or where they
lived. People often talk of the past in nostalgic terms,
calling them simpler times ("those were the days"), but
actually we humans have been wearing ourselves out
since the Fall in the Garden of Eden.

Kings are no exception. David surely felt worn out
repeatedly. His words in Psalm 23 are like balm to the
spent spirit. When we feel like we have to keep running at
a frantic pace just to meet the demands placed on us, it is
freeing to read that God "lets" us rest in green meadows.

Quiet yourself right now. What do you hear? Can you feel the soft breeze of that calm meadow? God gives us permission to rest! Then He leads us by peaceful streams, and in the process He renews our strength.

No matter how busy life is, God gives us permission to get away with Him and enjoy His rest. That may happen in five minutes or fifty, but He is capable of giving all of us the rest we need today.

• • • • • • • • • •

READ PSALM 23. THANK JESUS CHRIST FOR GIVING US PERMISSION TO REST IN HIM. HE KNOWS WE NEED IT, SO GO AHEAD AND TAKE A BREAK TODAY—WITH NO GUILT!

# Daily Dose of God's Word

*People do not live by bread alone, but by every word
that comes from the mouth of God.* Matthew 4:4

These days there seems to be a vitamin for anyone
whose body needs a boost! Vitamin D, omega-3, $B_3$,
$B_6$, $B_{12}$—the variety of vitamins and nutrients available
can be mind-boggling. Manufacturers promise they'll
help heal the heart, the kidneys, the immune system,
and the gut, for starters. There are even vitamins for
stronger nails.

Jesus is very clear in today's verse that bread and
water are not really enough for the kind of living that
makes for real health—physically, mentally, socially, and
spiritually. Just as vitamin supplements add healthy components to our physical diet, God's Word adds vitality to
our spiritual diet: "People do not live by bread alone, but
by every word that comes from the mouth of God."

This truth should encourage us not only today, but
every day. God is our Sustainer, the sustenance for our
souls. He offers us full access to Himself, and He speaks
to us through His Word, knowing His Word will serve
as spiritual nourishment.

I don't know about you, but when I forget to eat or

do not eat the right kinds of food, I get a headache and start to feel sluggish. Just get me an iced tea, cheese and crackers, nuts, beef jerky, and chocolate for my antioxidants, and I perk up.

Jesus tells us in Matthew 4:4 that Scripture sustains us. More than just a quick snack, it offers us lasting satisfaction and strength. The Lord used Scripture to battle temptation against Satan when He was physically famished. If Jesus—God Himself—used Scripture, we need to be digesting what He has to say in daily portions!

His power and obedience to His Word are exactly what we need to survive the onslaught from the enemy and from our own weaknesses. His Word leaves us satisfied, strong, and ready for battle!

. . . . . . . . . .

LET'S READ 1 PETER 2:2-3 AS A REMINDER OF OUR NEED FOR DAILY NOURISHMENT AND PUT IT INTO PRACTICE IN THE POWER OF THE HOLY SPIRIT. IT'S HOW WE HEAR HIS VOICE!

# 52

## You Have One Job!

*Worry weighs a person down; an encouraging
word cheers a person up.* Proverbs 12:25

When I received the unexpected bad news of having
breast cancer, my main heartache was my impressionable
twelve-year-old daughter watching the ordeal of cancer
from the sidelines. I did *not* want her to worry, and I
did not want to miss being there for her wedding day
someday in the future. I did not want to be away from
home and unavailable to greet her as she came home
from middle school.

I will never forget hugging Kali in the foyer before
my mastectomy. In fact, God has continually used this
particular mother-daughter interaction in both our
lives. Many years have passed since that day, yet it still
seems as fresh as yesterday. As we were saying our good-
byes, I looked at her and said, "You have one job while
Mommy is away."

She looked at me with those beautiful, almost-
teenager eyes and rolled them as if to ask, "Do I have
to empty the dishwasher, vacuum, and blow the leaves
off the back porch?"

Catching her nonverbal response, I said, "No, your
only job is *not to worry*! You see, Mommy is in the best

hands possible—the Lord's. So are you and Daddy. And I am not afraid because I will not be alone, and God loves me and you and Daddy more than we can imagine. As a mother with 'crazy love' for her beautiful daughter, my biggest fear is that you will be worried about me! I want you to enjoy your school and friends and your dad while I am in the hospital. I want to *not worry* about you because that will be much harder for me than the mastectomy!"

She got the biggest smile on her face. Every now and then in the days that followed I would ask her how she was doing with her job. It became our thing—*no worries!* God gave both of us courage in cancer *not to worry!*

· · · · · · · · · ·

CAN YOU NAME THE BIGGEST WORRY OF YOUR LIFE? WRITE IT DOWN, THEN WRITE THE WORDS OF PROVERBS 12:25 OVER IT. GOD DOES NOT WANT HIS CHILDREN TO WORRY.

# 53

# Put on God's Armor

*Put on every piece of God's armor so you will be able
to resist the enemy in the time of evil. . . . Stand your
ground, putting on the belt of truth and the body armor
of God's righteousness. For shoes, put on the peace that
comes from the Good News. . . . Hold up the shield
of faith to stop the fiery arrows of the devil. Put on
salvation as your helmet, and take the sword of the
Spirit, which is the word of God.* Ephesians 6:13-17

What are you wearing today? Maybe it's one of your
favorite outfits or maybe it is the first thing you grabbed
that didn't need ironing. Some women, like me, enjoy
creating new looks and shopping in their own closets to
stay in touch with the current styles. But today's verses
focus on the real essentials needed to dress for success.

God's wardrobe for us—His armor—may not seem
to fit your fashion style, but we would be wise not to
leave the house without it. This outerwear is actually our
innerwear, protecting us from the enemy and helping
us defend God's truth and stand our ground. Here's
what's included:

**Belt of truth:** Truth guards our core against the onslaught
of misleading standards.

**Body armor of righteousness:** God's righteousness covers our whole being.

**Shoes of peace:** The Good News gives us peace, and we can share the story of the Prince of Peace with others.

**Shield of faith:** Faith protects us like a shield over our heart, where Jesus resides when we have a relationship with Him.

**Helmet of salvation:** Jesus' death secured our salvation, and when we focus on that fact, we don helmets of confidence for what lies ahead.

**Sword of the Spirit:** The Word of God is our only offensive piece of armor. When we carry the sword of the Spirit, we'll be ready to wage war against the enemy using the power of God's Word.

• • • • • • • • • •

AS YOU DRESS EACH DAY, THINK OF EACH PIECE OF SPIRITUAL ARMOR YOU'RE PUTTING ON TOO. THEN LISTEN TO WHAT OUR COMMANDER IN CHIEF, JESUS, ASKS YOU TO DO AND WEAR HIM WELL!

# 54

## Sheer Delight

*He led me to a place of safety; he rescued me*
*because he delights in me.* 2 Samuel 22:20

When I was in third or fourth grade, I remember
a particularly delightful surprise at my first sleepover
birthday party. I invited a group of girls to bring their
own pillows and sleeping bags and spend the night.
Little did I know when we awoke the next morning
that my mom and dad would scoop us all into the car
*with our pajamas on* and drive us twenty minutes away
to have ice-cream sundaes for breakfast. Now that was
a delight!

When I turn once again to my trusty children's
dictionary, I learn that the word *delight* means "great
pleasure." Did you know that God delights in His children? Because He is the same yesterday, today, tomorrow, and for all eternity, God has always delighted in
each one of us and always will. Wow! Put your name in
the blank and see how meaningful that is: God delighted
in _____ before she was born, and God
delights in _____ now. God will delight
in _____ forever! I don't know about you,
but that almost makes me squeal aloud.

When we delight in someone, we long for that

person. This longing creates a desire to spend time together. That describes God's desire toward us.

Dwell on this truth today and every day: God takes great pleasure in you and me. Jesus took great pleasure in saving us, despite His pain and separation from His heavenly Father while on the cross. He still takes great pleasure in being with us—in growing, restoring, healing, and loving us and offering us grace and truth— no matter our past, our present, or our future. His delight toward us is steadfast. It bubbles up in our souls and helps us delight in Him right back.

● ● ● ● ● ● ● ● ● ●

TREAT A FRIEND TO SOMETHING SWEET, WHETHER
IT'S EDIBLE OR NOT. BE DELIGHTED TODAY
THAT GOD DELIGHTS IN YOU AND ME!

# 55

# The Three Rs

*I tell you the truth, unless you are born again,
you cannot see the Kingdom of God.* John 3:3

Even though I'm a former schoolteacher, I am not referring to the well-known three Rs associated with education: *r*eading, *w*riting, and a*r*ithmetic. I am thinking about a different set of three Rs: *R*eborn and *R*econstructed because of the *R*esurrection!

Once we are reborn spiritually through Christ, we spend the rest of our lives on this earth being reconstructed to look more like Him. It's only because of His resurrection that we are able to be reborn and receive resurrected bodies when our earthly ones die.

The actual resurrection of Jesus from the grave is the most important fact in history. At first, even Jesus' disciples, His closest friends, didn't believe what had happened. But when they were convinced that He was alive again, they began to experience His spiritual reconstruction that molded their character and strengthened their faith. They became rock-solid followers of Jesus who shared with individuals and crowds the good news of salvation and eternal life. Thousands believed and died to defend that belief. Because of the three Rs, we have:

- *Assurance of eternal life.* Disease and death can't take it away from us.
- *Hope.* What we are experiencing now isn't all there is to life. There is so much more to look forward to in our eternal home in heaven with the Lord.
- *Protection and provision.* God protects and meets the needs of His children.
- *Abundant life.* No matter what difficulties we are dealing with, God provides joy and peace smack-dab in the middle of them all!
- *Companionship.* We are His and He is ours!

These promises are ours, given to us by the world's greatest Teacher, who still lives—Jesus.

. . . . . . . . . . .

REMEMBER THE THREE Rs. WE ARE BEING REBORN AND RECONSTRUCTED, AND WE WILL ONE DAY BE RESURRECTED!

# 56

# Our Comforter

*"Comfort, comfort my people," says your God. . . .*
*Have you never heard? Have you never understood?*
*The LORD is the everlasting God, the Creator of all*
*the earth. He never grows weak or weary. No one can*
*measure the depths of his understanding. He gives*
*power to the weak and strength to the powerless. Even*
*youths will become weak and tired, and young men*
*will fall in exhaustion. But those who trust in the*
*LORD will find new strength. They will soar high on*
*wings like eagles. They will run and not grow weary.*
*They will walk and not faint.* Isaiah 40:1, 28-31

My heart hurts. Last night I went to bed upset about
something, and this morning I awakened with the same
splinter lodged in my heart. I'm sure you know what
a hurt heart feels like! I think I'd trade this ache for a
broken bone any day. At least then I could go to a clinic
and get medical attention. Being assured that the healing
process was in motion would ease my anxiety, knowing
how and when that bone would be restored.

We can look at a physical injury and assess what
it will take to mend it, and we can use X-rays or other
diagnostic imagery to figure out what's wrong. But hurts
of the heart are often invisible and difficult to diagnose,

much less to heal. Even counseling has its limitations for healing.

Only God can reach down into a person's heart and bathe it with cleansing balm that cleans the wound and brings comfort. No human therapy can thoroughly remove emotional pain and replace it with wholeness like God can.

Every emotion that we can ever feel and every hurt we can ever imagine has been experienced by Jesus. He comforts us throughout His Word by reminding us of His presence and plan for restoring us.

Isaiah 40 is packed with Jesus' healing balm for our wounds. Go to the everlasting God, the Creator of the earth and of every human heart, for comfort that only He can give.

. . . . . . . . . .

NEED COMFORT FOR YOUR HURTING HEART?
OPEN YOUR BIBLE TO ISAIAH 40 AND READ ABOUT
GOD'S COMFORT FOR HURTING HEARTS.

# 57

# Daily Pep Talk

*Let us strip off every weight that slows us down,
especially the sin that so easily trips us up. And let us
run with endurance the race God has set before us.
We do this by keeping our eyes on Jesus, the champion
who initiates and perfects our faith.* Hebrews 12:1-2

I need this pep talk from God every day, don't you? We
are all running this race of life not knowing how long it
will last, how many losses we will face, or if any earthly
cheerleaders will ever show up by our side.

Life is full of unknowns, yet the clock is ticking and
our choice for survival is faith in Christ, our true Life
Coach. He has already won the eternal life "race" for
us, so our goal really isn't about winning eternal life but
about living by faith.

I love His practical advice here in Hebrews 12. When
I get dressed every morning, I literally cut off every weight
that slows me down—those tags in my blouses that itch
the back of my neck, those ribbons stitched into the
shoulders to keep your clothes on the hanger but that
always manage to hang out when you don't notice. And
pockets? I have most of them cut out and tightly sewn
up because if I put anything in them, they literally bog
me down with added weight to my thighs!

Jesus requires us to throw off anything—especially our sin—that slows us down from progressing in our faith. The very best way to live is to remain fixed on our constant, Jesus Christ. Life and faith are simpler if we are not holding on to anything that holds us back from Jesus. Focusing on Jesus in the race He sets for you and me is a game changer for sure!

* * * * * * * * * *

NEED A DAILY PEP TALK? KEEP YOUR EYES ON JESUS AND GET RID OF ANYTHING THAT DISTRACTS YOU FROM YOUR PRIMARY FOCUS, WHICH IS JESUS HIMSELF!

# 58

# Generous God-Givers

*Everything we have has come from you, and
we give you only what you first gave us!*
1 Chronicles 29:14

Although not everything I've ever done may be
described as logical, this truth about giving is very
logical: We can be generous God-givers to a depleted
world because nothing really belongs to us. We freely
give what God has lavished on us. His giving nature
is a primary motivation for us to follow His lead and
become givers ourselves.

No human can motivate us to do anything like God
can! I'm sure someone has said somewhere that God's
Word is the only self-help book we need. It should be
on the top of our book stack, worn from use! His Word
motivates me like no other book does.

Whether the Lord wants to urge us to give, to clean,
to forgive, to go the extra mile, to cook, to call, to write,
to exercise, to commit, or to change by the power of
His Spirit, God prompts us through His Word. But we
need to sensitize our hearts to listen for His direction
and then accept His nudge to act on that gentle push
He gives us. Every time I have personally held back
from giving something, I have regretted it. Haven't you?

We need to develop the doer aspect of giving and move beyond merely dreaming of the possibilities.

The fact that everything we have belongs to Him should motivate us to not hold back. If we have a resource, whatever it is—not just money, but time and talents as well—we just need to let it go! When we give to people, we give to God and we point others to Him, the best Gift Giver there is.

• • • • • • • • • •

LET'S BE GENEROUS WITH ALL GOD'S GIFTS. HE GAVE THEM TO US SO THAT WE WOULD PASS THEM ON TO OTHERS AS A WAY TO SHARE HIS GENEROUS LOVE.

# 59

# How Are Your Relationships?

*[Jesus] answered, "'Love the Lord your God with*
*all your heart and with all your soul and with*
*all your strength and with all your mind'; and,*
*'Love your neighbor as yourself.'"* Luke 10:27, NIV

When it comes to marketing, Hallmark knows what to do. Their cards are all about wonderful ways to make connections with other people. You can even share your card story on their website. And then there are the commercials! They always make me cry because they draw me into what life is really about—relationships. The relationship between a mother and daughter, a teacher and student, one friend to another.

How are we doing in our relationships? Let's think about it. If you and I have an altercation with someone and do not do our part to resolve it, are we at peace? Of course not. We are either stewing at work or stewing at home, and heaven forbid, we may have gossiped about it to someone, and started that person stewing too.

Sweet friends, God set our priorities in Luke 10:27 with the two most important commandments—to love Him and to love people. If our relationships with God and people are full of strife or are simply lacking, then we need to do a heart check to see if our love priorities are in order.

If we have a personal relationship with God through Christ, we need to ask ourselves if we love Him with all our heart, soul, strength, and mind. If we do, then we should have greater love for others. As our relationship with God grows and we come to love Him more, in His strength and power He moves us toward restoration and reconciliation in our earthly relationships. We will not have time to look critically at others and judge them because our relationship with our holy, gracious God keeps our hearts softened. When we live in light of God's perfect, infinite grace, forgiveness, and mercy with our own failings, then we will want to do what we can to offer grace and forgiveness to others rather than pushing to win an argument and get our way.

When we keep our relationship with God on His terms, it will carry over to our relationships with others.

. . . . . . . . . .

LET'S GROW IN OUR LOVE FOR THE LORD, AND ALL OUR OTHER RELATIONSHIPS WILL GROW AND BLOSSOM TOO.

# 60

# Pleasant Words

*Pleasant words are a honeycomb, sweet to the soul
and healing to the bones.* Proverbs 16:24, NASB

The Bible's proverbs are so practical! This was the proverb I read during my "Be still, and know that I am God" quiet time today.

I had to laugh when I read the phrase "healing to the bones" in Proverbs 16:24 because my annual bone-density exam was this very same day! A bone-density test is an easy screening. You lie still while a magnetic shield passes over your body and records your bone density. Just like that, a lot of information about your bones gets recorded, printed out, and sent to the doctor, who goes over the results later with you.

While this test is effective in providing helpful information, it has no healing power and is not nearly as fun as pleasant words. We all know what they feel like: gracious . . . kind . . . uncondemning. God can use pleasant words to lift the spirit of even the most critically ill patient. As destructive as the tongue can be, pleasant words are much more powerful!

Recently my family members (including me) slipped into a habit of not carefully filtering our tone or editing the words we were saying to each other. We all fell into the pattern of letting less-than-gracious words slide off our tongues—words that did not feel sweet to the soul or healing to the bones.

Words are so powerful. That's why reading God's Word is so life changing. We receive genuine encouragement through these holy and God-breathed words. In the Bible we learn how to develop speech patterns that honor God and others.

. . . . . . . . . .

AS WE LISTEN TO GOD'S PLEASANT WORDS, LET'S CONSIDER WHAT GENUINE, PLEASANT WORDS WE CAN USE TO ENCOURAGE OTHERS!

# 61

# We Have an Advocate

*My dear children, I am writing this to you so that you will not sin. But if anyone does sin, we have an advocate who pleads our case before the Father. He is Jesus Christ, the one who is truly righteous.* 1 John 2:1

Don't you love it when someone stands up for you and watches your back? We are so appreciative of the people God puts in our lives who go the extra mile to defend and encourage us—people who really step up for us in difficult situations.

There is no escaping trouble in this wounded world. Even for those who have walked wholeheartedly with the Lord for many years, sin is not a stranger. The fact that everyone in Christ has an advocate—Jesus Christ Himself, the One who is truly righteous—is worth celebrating today and every day. His presence provides a sweet place of grace where we can go when we sin.

God sees our case through the cross of Christ. We no longer face a prosecutor because the defense team of Jesus has won every case of the accused who have chosen Him by faith. It's the only way to stand before our righteous Judge—God Almighty! But sometimes we forget our Advocate.

All of us have a go-between, Someone who literally

steps in and always goes to bat for us. His name is Jesus. He is the go-between who reconciles a holy God and our sinful selves. He makes the way for us to have a personal relationship with God.

Our personal Advocate—our way to God—is always interceding on our behalf. No perfect person on earth can do this for us—only Jesus!

. . . . . . . . . .

TAKE HEART. YOU HAVE A PERSONAL ADVOCATE WHO IS ALWAYS RIGHT AND ALWAYS PULLING FOR YOU. PRAISE HIM FOR PERSONALLY HANDLING THE ACCUSATIONS AGAINST YOU FOR SIN. AND WHEN THAT GRACE GAVEL IS POUNDED ON GOD'S DESK OF MERCY, HE WILL PROCLAIM, "NOT GUILTY!"

# 62

# Go God!

*The LORD is faithful to all his promises and*
*loving toward all he has made. . . . The LORD*
*is righteous in all his ways and loving toward*
*all he has made.*  Psalm 145:13, 17, NIV

Let's celebrate today whether we feel up to it or not!
God wants to lift our hearts now.

Perhaps today you're feeling sad or unloved or
discouraged. Maybe you are wondering if anyone really
cares about you. Well, look with me at Psalm 145
and celebrate the Lord's greatness, just like His child
David did!

God's methods might seem a little unusual. He
could remove all of our troubles in an instant. But more
often He calls us to draw near to Him, and He lifts our
spirits as we celebrate Him.

Reading this psalm makes me feel like God's cheerleader. By the time I finish verse 21, I'm practically
shouting, "Go God!" No matter how I feel when I
begin, my heart is lifted as I echo David's words.

We have reason to praise the Lord because:

- He is the only One who knows us inside and out!
- He can be nothing but loving toward us.

- What He says goes. And we need to be glad it does because He is always right!
- He is faithful to all His promises!

We are reminded in this psalm that God is righteous and faithful in all His ways. No matter what you and I are facing or feeling right now, He is loving on us! We need to harness our faulty feelings and by faith remind ourselves of what we know is true.

God created us with feelings, but we don't want to make decisions based on feelings or have our feelings determine the outcome of our day. Let's base our emotions on what God says, knowing He always has our backs!

He is loving toward all He has made, which includes sweet you and me!

. . . . . . . . . . .

CONTINUE CELEBRATING GOD'S GREATNESS.
SPEND FIVE MINUTES LISTING THE WAYS GOD
HAS ACTED FAITHFULLY AND LOVINGLY
TOWARD YOU AND YOUR FAMILY.

# 63

# Sweet Tweet

*Calling the crowd to join his disciples, [Jesus] said, "If any of you wants to be my follower, you must turn from your selfish ways, take up your cross, and follow me."* Mark 8:34

If Jesus had a smartphone, I wonder if "Follow me" would have been His first tweet. It certainly fits within Twitter's character limits!

It's funny to think about Jesus pulling out His cell phone and typing that message, but you know, I believe He would do just that if He came to earth today. He met people where they were and connected with them in ways they understood. He would definitely be the master tweeter. I wonder how quickly His follower count would grow.

The crowd Jesus addresses in today's story was made up of people just like you and me who wanted to see for themselves what was going on with this man they had heard about. The news had spread about His miracles, like healing a deaf man and a blind man and feeding four thousand people with only seven loaves of bread and a few small fish. Not only did everyone there get more than enough to eat, but there were plenty of left-overs, too.

It is *amazing* how God can do so much with so little!

He can communicate volumes with very few words, and He can reach anyone, anywhere, without the power of social media. His ability to reach people at their point of need has always been more spectacular than any man-made media can achieve. I echo the disciple John when he said, "Jesus also did many other things. If they were all written down, I suppose the whole world could not contain the books that would be written" (John 21:25).

Jesus is worth following, and following closely. His messages to us are like sweet tweets that went viral long ago and still bear retweeting.

When I imagine a modern-day crowd all with cell phones listening to Jesus and receiving His sweet tweet invitation to follow Him, I hope everyone is tweeting back, "Yes! I'll follow" and then retweeting it to all their friends.

* * * * * * * * * *

RETWEET: #FollowJesus. Or respond
to His sweet tweet today.

127

# 64

# A Feast Every Day

*When I discovered your words, I devoured them. They are my joy and my heart's delight, for I bear your name, O Lord God of Heaven's Armies.* Jeremiah 15:16

There is an old saying that goes, "When faith goes to market, it always takes a basket." I like that. Faith moves. It requires action, even if it means we must wait.

There is nothing complicated about the Christian life—unless we let our human perspectives and weaknesses clutter our hearts and edge out the space rightfully reserved for God. Through the power of Jesus Christ, faith in Him is the simplest, least burdensome way to live! His Word, the Bible, tells us what that looks like.

In Deuteronomy 32:46-47, Moses said to God's children, the Israelites, "Take to heart all the words of warning I have given you today. Pass them on as a command to your children so they will obey every word of these instructions. These instructions are not empty words—they are your life! By obeying them you will enjoy a long life in the land you will occupy when you cross the Jordan River."

I'll take the liberty of modernizing the quote that began this devotion: "When faith goes to the grocery store, it always gets a cart." Before I go to the grocery store, I always make a list of the things I need to pick up for our weekly meals. I drive to the store, select a grocery cart, choose my items, and place them in the cart. I have never been grocery shopping without putting something in my cart.

Living by faith requires that we pick up the Word of God and actually put His promises in our personal grocery carts. When we practice this habit on a daily basis, our appetites will grow to want more of Him. When we want more of Him, we'll be motivated to do things His way and act in faith to move in His direction and not our own.

REMEMBER THAT GOD'S WORD IS *NONPERISHABLE*, AND HIS WORDS ARE AS LIFE-SUSTAINING AS THE FOOD WE EAT. FEASTING ON HIS GOODNESS SHARPENS OUR CRAVING FOR MORE OF HIM.

# Eternal Report Cards

*But to all who believed him and accepted him, he gave the right to become children of God.* John 1:12

When I was teaching school, every year I wanted to quit the day I had to hand out report cards. Of course, I knew that evaluation was important, but marking in little black boxes on a report card could never show some of the special, delightful qualities of each child! Even though I filled up the space allotted for hand-written comments, I know everyone considered an A as "very good," and most girls, more so than boys, thought a C was very bad. Ds and Fs were much worse news for both boys and girls!

Grades really mattered to the children, thus they mattered to me. Although I was careful in my evaluations, I constantly wondered how to keep "my children" from thinking a report card was the total evaluation of them as a person. I longed for them to know their value was based on how much God loved them. More than anything, in my heart I wanted them to grasp God's acceptance of them. Knowing Jesus Christ means we receive an A+ on our eternal report card!

Who is our teacher? Our teacher is God Almighty, and His learning curve takes into account our unique strengths and weaknesses. He knows the ideal teaching strategy for each of His children. His methods are encouraging; He adapts them according to His purpose for us.

As students of our Savior, we are called to study His Word and follow His curriculum. This discipline becomes a joy because we learn to love and respect God so much as we experience what a wonderful, caring teacher He is. And someday when He deems the timing is right, we will graduate to heaven forever.

Wow! I just encouraged myself writing this and reminding myself what is true!

· · · · · · · · · ·

IF YOU HAVE GIVEN YOUR LIFE TO CHRIST (YOU CAN DO THAT RIGHT NOW IF YOU HAVEN'T—JUST TELL HIM), CELEBRATE YOUR A+ IN JESUS AND GET EXCITED ABOUT WHAT HE HAS IN STORE FOR YOU.

# 66

# Tooth Tale

*O LORD, there is no one like you. We have never even heard of another God like you!* 1 Chronicles 17:20

When our daughter, Kali, started kindergarten, it was such a fun time around our house. She was so excited about starting school and getting a new backpack. And after the first day, she couldn't stop talking about the tooth chart in her classroom. Whenever anyone lost a tooth, his or her name was added to the chart and everyone celebrated!

One morning when Mark was getting ready for work, Kali said to me, "Mommy, will you please pull my tooth? I'm afraid it's going to come out at school and I'll lose it. I want to be on the tooth chart." Inside I'm thinking, *I don't like blood. I wish Mark could pull it. There's no time.* Out loud I said, "Okay, sweet one," and wrapped one end of a piece of string around the loose tooth and tied the other end to the doorknob, my daddy's tried-and-true method.

Just then Mark appeared and said, "What are you doing? You may do that in South Carolina, but we don't do that in Virginia!" Needless to say, we had run out of time, and Kali went to school with her tooth still hanging on.

When she got home that day, our plumber, Mr. Trexler, strolled into the kitchen after fixing a leak under Kali's bathroom sink. He and his wife had a lot of children, so when he saw her wiggling her tooth, he said, "Do you want me to pull it for you?"

"Yes," she replied cheerfully, while I'm thinking, *Maybe you should wash your hands first!*

Mr. Trexler quickly grabbed a paper towel and yanked gently. Suddenly, Kali was grinning with a noticeable gap where the tooth had been. She drew a picture of herself smiling—without a tooth—to thank him. Later she asked, "Could Mr. Trexler come back and pull all my teeth? Nobody can do it just like him!" Tears of joy welled up in my eyes.

Doesn't that describe God, too? After all, nobody can do it just like God!

. . . . . . . . . . .

## WHAT SMALL THING DO YOU NEED TO PLACE IN GOD'S HANDS RIGHT NOW? TAKE A MOMENT AND PRAYERFULLY GIVE IT TO HIM TOO.

# 67

# His Favor Rests on Us

*Glory to God in the highest heaven, and on earth peace
to those on whom his favor rests.* Luke 2:14, NIV

Every Christmas morning when I was growing up,
my mom or dad read the Christmas story from Luke 2.
Sometimes I tuned out the all-too-familiar words, causing
them to skid off my heart rather than take root. Because
I had heard them so often, I neglected to appreciate the
meaning those words always bring to each holiday season.

When we hear something over and over again, we
sometimes become deaf to what is being said. But repetition is necessary and helpful for remembering truth.
God's Word never gets old and is worth reviewing over
and over again. It is full of repeated messages of God's
love, grace, care, and redemption for lost people. It is
alive and powerful (Hebrews 4:12). Amazingly, His
Word can set the tone for all that is going to take place
today, tomorrow, and forever. It's really as if God's Word
follows us around throughout the day.

To read it daily brings delight because no matter
how many times we read a passage, God's Spirit makes
His Word fresh in the hearts of all His children who are
sensitive to His voice. Our hearts become tender when

we know what God says, and we not only want to live by it but we actually *do* what He says by faith. This is called obedience.

This past Christmas, God showed me fresh truth in the familiar verse Luke 2:14. He clearly reminded me that His favor rests on *me*! What a wonderful thought.

God approves of me in Christ Jesus. I do not have to win His favor or approval because He already proved His love and favor toward me by sending Christ into the world. On that first Christmas Jesus came to earth as a baby so we could experience God in human form.

God's favor rests on you, too—forever. Let the deep meaning of the Christmas story move your heart closer to His heart each and every day.

• • • • • • • • • •

LET'S LIVE LIKE WE ARE FAVORED! THANK
THE LORD THAT HIS WORD ALWAYS OFFERS
SOMETHING FRESH, LIKE THE STORY OF JESUS'
BIRTH. READ THE ACCOUNT IN LUKE 2:1-20.

# 68

# Splashes of Glory

*The heavens declare the glory of God; the skies proclaim the work of his hands.* Psalm 19:1, NIV

Soon after I completed the onslaught of my cancer treatments, Mark took our family on a gift trip to Hawaii. We had a wonderful time, and before we left the island to return home, he asked me if there was anything I really wanted to do before I left.

"Yes," I replied. "I want an adventure. I want to swim with the dolphins in the deep blue ocean, their natural habitat in the wild." I had seen an advertisement for this excursion in the touristy paraphernalia at the airport. Kali thought it was an exciting way to end our celebratory trip. So with a few pink butterflies fluttering in our stomachs, I called and signed us up.

The boat was big enough to hold six people, but our family was the only one that showed up that day. (Mark was with us, too, staying dry and watching us from the boat.) It was like having our own private adventure. The guide stopped the boat near a pod of at least two hundred spinner dolphins, which he admitted was an unusually large number and sighting.

As Kali and I glided in the warm water with face masks and snorkels, we felt as if we were the only two land mammals in the entire ocean. It was like God arranged it for just the two of us! We were having so much fun in Awe Land that we stayed in the ocean three hours. We did not break for lunch and did not care that our sunscreen wore out long before we did.

The experience was worth every second and every inch of sunburn because it gave us a chance to see a fascinating part of God's wondrous creation up close and personal. We couldn't help but worship Him alongside His beautiful aquatic creatures.

*The dolphins declare the glory of God!* kept running through my mind. I saw the glory of God through my face mask as He let me experience one of His top ten wonders on my personal worship list!

. . . . . . . . . .

"THE HEAVENS DECLARE THE GLORY OF GOD." THE DOLPHINS DO TOO! IF YOU NEED A FRESH DOSE OF GOD'S GLORY, GO TO A ZOO, WALK ON A NATURE TRAIL, SPEND A DAY AT THE BEACH, OR SIMPLY EAT LUNCH OUTSIDE. AND BY ALL MEANS, LOOK UP!

# 69

# Acquiring God's Taste

*Don't just pretend to love others. Really love
them. Hate what is wrong. Hold tightly
to what is good.* Romans 12:9

Good taste is something I always want to have. However, sometimes when my creative juices are flowing, I
can veer toward tacky, like using way too many "sweets"
in my writing or too much pink in one place. There is
nothing wrong with sweet pink, but there's something
to be said for tasteful moderation. I appreciate the good
taste of others so much—Sweet Faye's thoughtful gifts,
Sweet Debbie's web smarts, and my sweet daughter's
fashion sense.

When it comes to bigger issues of life, I want to
strive for God's taste because His is always very good. In
Romans 12:9, we see that God's taste is to love others,
hate what is wrong, and hold tightly to what is good.

Over time, God develops our taste for what pleases
Him as we conform to the image of Christ. Early in my
faith journey, I had a lot to learn about discernment.
Through the years, as I've gotten to know God personally through His Word, my conscience is pricked more
about what is His taste and what is not.

If you are thinking now about whether or not some

things in your own life reflect God's taste, that means the Holy Spirit is at work in you. That's a very, very good thing!

If we want God's taste reflected in our lives, we need to love people, hate what is wrong, and hold tightly to what is good.

* * * * * * * * * *

IF WE REMOVE ONE LITTLE "O" FROM THE WORD *GOOD*, WE GET *GOD*. GOD AND GOOD ARE INSEPARABLE BECAUSE GOD IS ALWAYS GOOD AND THERE IS NO REAL GOOD APART FROM GOD!

# 70

# Habakkuk's Heart

*Even though the fig trees have no blossoms, and there are no grapes on the vines; even though the olive crop fails, and the fields lie empty and barren; even though the flocks die in the fields, and the cattle barns are empty, yet I will rejoice in the LORD! I will be joyful in the God of my salvation! The Sovereign LORD is my strength!* Habakkuk 3:17-19

Habakkuk had a "cup half full" perspective on life—his empty cup overflowed!

At first glance we wonder how Habakkuk could have had such a great outlook. It appears as though he and the rest of the people lived in desperate circumstances, with little to no source of income or food for their next meal. But he knew life ahead was secured by God, even though the current environment looked bleak and resources were scarce. Habakkuk focused his heart on God and trusted that the Lord would see them through seemingly impossible circumstances.

Just as God's people had everything to look forward to in that situation, we have everything indescribably glorious to look forward to now! Our lot is sure. Yes, these days may be very difficult, with unknowns looming before us at every turn. It is tempting for us to curl up in fear or give in to discouragement and fatigue.

But one day we will see the Lord face to face and never know need again! We will never hurt or cry again. We will have glorious new bodies and a new home in heaven forever with Him. No matter what you and I or the people we love are facing at this very moment, no matter what fills our list of *even though*s, we still have the most amazing reason to rejoice.

Let's you and I list our own personal *even though*s—

- *Even though* I just lost my spouse, home, health, job, savings . . .
- *Even though* I can't have a baby . . .
- *Even though* I'm going through a divorce . . .
- *Even though* a serious illness lingers . . .

*Even though* my future seems hopeless, "yet I will rejoice in the LORD!"

. . . . . . . . . .

"LORD, PLEASE GIVE ME A HABAKKUK HEART."
POUR OUT YOUR LIST OF *EVEN THOUGH*S TO GOD
AND, BY FAITH, OFFER HIM PRAISE ANYWAY!

# 71

# Grace Gratefulness

*He said to me, "My grace is sufficient for you,*
*for my power is made perfect in weakness."*
*Therefore I will boast all the more gladly*
*about my weaknesses, so that Christ's power*
*may rest on me.* 2 Corinthians 12:9, NIV

Whenever I read the Bible and feel God shed His bright light on a dingy area in my life, my "grace gratefulness" to Him increases. I realize I fall short of His perfect standard, but I am encouraged that I have company. The Bible is full of stories about God extending His grace to people who did or said the wrong things.

I'm especially guilty when it comes to saying what's on my mind, often without thinking. James, the half brother of Jesus, has a lot to say about the tongue in his writings. He compares our tongues to tiny sparks that can set great forests on fire (James 3:5). If you have been to places that have been ravaged by fire or seen news reports about them, it's heartbreaking. Our unfiltered words can sear a person's heart in the same way. My tendency at times is a quick response, and this is why I identify with the apostle Peter's impulsiveness. I am glad God knows us so well and uses the approach of grace to change our weaknesses into strengths, just as He did with Peter.

Peter spoke and acted impulsively, but Jesus still loved him. Peter did not stop to think before he denied Jesus three times in a row, yet Jesus forgave Peter. As Peter grew in spiritual maturity, I'm guessing he also felt a lot of grace gratefulness.

God Almighty's way of personally relating with His followers who keep blowing it increases my grace gratefulness. God is always showing us mercy as He changes us to better reflect His good character. I've come to understand how much I need His grace, which He lavishes on His own. The more I love Him, the more I want to please Him and the more my grace gratefulness grows.

There is no way to ever be snatched from God's hand. His grace grips us in every area of our lives, including our tongues. God's grace frees us from being paralyzed by guilt when we sin. Let's not waste a minute wallowing in guilt. Jesus told us if we confess our sin, He "is faithful and just to forgive us our sins and to cleanse us from all wickedness" (1 John 1:9).

⬤ ⬤ ⬤ ⬤ ⬤ ⬤ ⬤ ⬤ ⬤ ⬤

# WHAT SWEET ENCOURAGEMENT TO ALL OF US. READ JEREMIAH 15:16.

# 72

# He Has Your Back

*Joshua conquered all these kings and their land
in a single campaign, for the LORD, the God of
Israel, was fighting for his people.* Joshua 10:42

Most of us have heard it said on television or in a
movie battle scene. One soldier says to another, "Don't
worry. I've got your back." It's a statement meant to
dispel fear and boost courage in crisis or danger. Kali
said this to me before I stepped off a mountain for a *very*
high-ropes mother/daughter adventure.

How blessed the Lord's people are that our Heavenly
Commander has our backs. And just so we'll be absolutely secure, He also goes before us into every battle.
He knows the winning tactics, and He leads us through
the fight, no matter how difficult the terrain or the
depth of darkness we find ourselves in.

Isn't it comforting to know that we have an invin-
cible Father who is also our Warrior and our Protector?
He always has our best interests at heart. He knows we
are weak soldiers made of dust, and He even understands that sometimes in our panic or confusion we
push against Him instead of leaning into Him. Even
then, He still loves us. When we submit to His strate-
gies and authority, we can march throughout life's

circumstances empowered by His Spirit in ways we may never even see to fight life's battles.

And to top it off, *He always wins.* Not only is He undefeated, but *He is undefeatable.* No matter what, we are always on the winning side. When we take our marching orders from the true Commander in Chief and we stay on His path, follow His orders, and allow Him to fight for us, we are assured of ultimate victory. That's a battle plan worth defending!

. . . . . . . . . .

LET'S COMMIT TODAY TO FIGHT OUR BATTLES WITH GOD, NOT AGAINST HIM, LEANING INTO HIM FOR SUPPORT. WHEN WE SAY, "YES SIR, LORD" TO EVERYTHING, WE ARE ASSURED OF ULTIMATE SWEET VICTORY!

# 73

# Be a Cheerleader

*Encourage each other and build each other up,*
*just as you are already doing.* 1 Thessalonians 5:11

I loved being a cheerleader in middle school, high school, and college. Early on, my sweet mama told me that I couldn't be a cheerleader all my life. She knew the kind of commitment it took. But this is probably the only time Mama's been proven wrong.

You see, I'm married to a wonderful schoolteacher and coach, so I'm always cheering for his basketball and tennis players as well as the team representing his alma mater! As a mother, my cheerleading responsibilities have doubled. Even though I don't always jump up at the right time, I try to let my husband and daughter know in different ways that I'm always on their team.

One way to "cheer" for my family is to care about the things they care about. My sweet mother taught me this gracious principle by example. I remember as a middle-school student telling her about my eyebrows growing together. Instead of telling me to get over my bushy eyebrows, she immediately took action. She cared about what I cared about at a very self-conscious stage in my life. I've been indebted to her ever since!

Our world is full of negative people and

bullies—large and small. As daughters of our heavenly Father, we can practice His example and build up our family members first, then others. Each day we face many choices about whether to act as a "go girl" encourager or a "boo girl" discourager.

As believers in Christ, we are all on the same team, and we need to cheer for each other throughout this game of life. God so sweetens our lives through the genuine encouragement of others. We all need to practice our cheerleading skills and care!

＊ ＊ ＊ ＊ ＊ ＊ ＊ ＊ ＊ ＊

TODAY, LET'S ROOT FOR ONE OR TWO PEOPLE WHO COULD USE A BOOST OF ENCOURAGEMENT. SHOW YOU ARE INTERESTED IN WHAT THEY CARE ABOUT! PRAY FOR THEM, AND LET THEM KNOW THAT GOD PUT THEM ON YOUR HEART.

# 74

## A Fresh Supply of Mercy

*Yet I still dare to hope when I remember this:*
*The faithful love of the LORD never ends! His mercies*
*never cease. Great is his faithfulness; his mercies*
*begin afresh each morning.* Lamentations 3:21-23

We have a bread drawer in our kitchen, a deep drawer lined with stainless steel. The drawer was there when we moved into the house, and I had no idea what it was until I asked someone.

At times, I actually forget that I store bread in there because it is hidden away. When I finally remember it's there, I always hurry to pull it out before Mark finds the mold on it! Unfortunately, this week I wasn't fast enough, and he found it first. I told him that it was a good thing—we didn't need to eat all those carbohydrates anyway!

You and I do not order stale, moldy bread at our favorite sandwich shop, and we do not eat rotten meat. We like our food fresh, and for good reason. Food past its prime is distasteful and can even make us sick.

As much as I enjoy fresh food, I am perpetually grateful for fresh mercy every day! How grateful I am to our faithful, loving God that I do not have to try to store up mercy, hide it in the bread drawer, and hope it doesn't grow moldy! Every day our faithful God offers a fresh supply of mercy, along with love and every good thing you and I could ever need for sustenance.

Fresh mercy is one of the most encouraging benefits of belonging to Jesus Christ. We don't have to hoard it. It arrives in abundance, ready to reenergize and restore us.

. . . . . . . . . .

PRAISE GOD THAT MERCY NEVER GETS MOLDY!
WE WAKE UP TO FRESH MERCY EACH DAY. LET'S
REMEMBER LAMENTATIONS 3:21-23 AS WE GO TO
SLEEP TONIGHT AND AGAIN TOMORROW WHEN WE
WAKE UP TO FRESH MERCY, JUST AS HE PROMISES!

# 75

# Heroes among Us

*Be happy with those who are happy, and weep
with those who weep.*  Romans 12:15

We all need Christian heroes this side of heaven to
model Jesus Christ. Being surrounded by so many heroes
in my life has helped me grow in my love for Christ.

Most of my close heroes have been women, simply
because I have only two men in my life whom I spend
time with: Jesus and my husband. But over the years
I have certainly learned much from people who have
shared God's wisdom through their books, sermons, and
occupations. The great men and women of faith in the
Bible are also heroes to me because God recorded His
words to us through them and they helped grow the
early church. We are all a part of that early church today
if we have trusted in Christ.

Anyone can be a hero of faith simply by living God's
way day by day. Oftentimes the ongoing stresses of the
mundane can try our faith more than a more intense but
short-lived trial. Everyday heroes is what Romans 12 is
about—practical ways God's people live the Christian
life as a living sacrifice to God.

As Christian brothers and sisters, we are recipients
of God's great love and mercy for us through each other.

Right now, think of someone who has sacrificed his or her time, spiritual gifts, or earthly treasures for you. In Romans 12:15 we are instructed by Paul to "be happy with those who are happy, and weep with those who weep." Being a faithful and available servant who ministers to others takes heroic strength, patience, unselfishness, and courage. Getting in the trenches and sharing someone's hardship shines Jesus' light and love over someone who needs Him.

My sweet friend Jayne has a card ministry. It is something God has given her to do. I am always amazed by her thoughtfulness toward others in the good times as well as the sad situations. You and I may not have this particular hero quality, but we can find our own style of reaching out. That's what branches do (John 15)!

* * * * * * * * * *

HAVE YOU EVER CONSIDERED YOUR POTENTIAL TO BE A HERO? YOU DON'T NEED A FANCY COSTUME OR SUPERPOWERS. YOUR POWER COMES FROM GOD HIMSELF. THINK OF A WAY TO GIVE OF YOURSELF TODAY AND BE A HERO IN THE LITTLE THINGS. GOD MAKES YOUR EFFORT BIG.

# 76

## We Can Do This

*Trust in the LORD and do good. Then you will live*
*safely in the land and prosper. Take delight in the*
*LORD, and he will give you your heart's desires. Commit*
*everything you do to the LORD. Trust him, and he*
*will help you. . . . Be still in the presence of the LORD,*
*and wait patiently for him to act. Don't worry about*
*evil people who prosper or fret about their wicked*
*schemes. Stop being angry! Turn from your rage!*
*Do not lose your temper—it only leads to harm.*
Psalm 37:3-5, 7-8

I'm a list maker. A list helps me remember things and
feel productive throughout the day. There's something
about checking things off a list that floats my pink boat!
When I make a list, I love putting a little box like this □
in front of the task or item so that I can check it off *and*
cross a big line through it!

The beginning of Psalm 37 lists wonderful practical
wisdom that I like to check off in my head, reminding me to submit to God's ways instead of going with
my natural tendencies. I don't rush through it; instead,
I pray and ask God to help me stick to what He says.
I'm so thankful that in His power, His list is possible to
accomplish. For example,

- ☐ I *can* trust in the Lord and commit everything I do to Him.
- ☐ I *can* be still in the presence of the Lord and wait patiently for Him to act.
- ☐ I *can* refuse to worry about the wicked or their schemes.
- ☐ I *can* stop being angry and losing my temper.

The instructions work together. For instance, when we wait patiently for the Lord to act and trust in Him, we have an easier time avoiding worry about evil people who prosper in their wicked schemes. When we still ourselves in the Lord, we take delight in Him and naturally want to commit our ways to Him, to do good, and to hold our temper.

In the Spirit's power, we can cross off all of these instructions daily. Then we can enjoy the blessings God offers each of us, including peace and joy.

. . . . . . . . . .

PRAY THROUGH THE PSALM 37 LIST TODAY AND ASK THE LORD FOR HIS STRENGTH TO HELP YOU LIVE HIS WAY.

# 77

## Learning Contentment

*True godliness with contentment is itself great wealth.*
*After all, we brought nothing with us when we came*
*into the world, and we can't take anything with us*
*when we leave it. So if we have enough food and*
*clothing, let us be content.* 1 Timothy 6:6-8

Can you think of five people right now who you know
are truly content? How about four? Three? Two? One? Is
contentment becoming a lost virtue?

From Philippians 4:11 we know that contentment
can be learned. But does our saturated society hinder
us from living in true contentment when it sends the
message that things we want are really things we need,
whether or not it's true? Are we really failing or passing
in this "learning contentment" education? Are we doing
any homework in this area?

When we read daily what God has to say in His
Word, we hear His voice and understand more clearly
what He is like. We also allow Him to fill us with more
of His Spirit, which gives us true fulfillment. Being with
the Lord grows contentment.

Reading today's verses, let's ask ourselves if we are
growing in godliness and contentment. Aside from
spending time with God, we can avoid areas that bring

us discontentment. Personally, sometimes I look at too many catalogs and then buy things I don't need. I am more content when I am budget conscious and keep my innate "need to shop" tendencies under control.

Comparing ourselves with others is a surefire route to being discontent, so let's avoid doing that. Discontentment will look different on each one of us, but godliness looks the same for all of us. God's Spirit will zero in where He wants each of us to take a step of faith in obedience to Him.

. . . . . . . . . .

JUMP-START LEARNING CONTENTMENT. WHAT IS CAUSING DISCONTENTMENT IN YOUR LIFE TODAY? RIGHT NOW, REST IN YOUR PRESENT CIRCUMSTANCES AS A CHILD OF A PERFECT GOD.

# 78

# God's Word Is Always in Style

*You must love the LORD your God with all your heart, all
your soul, and all your strength. And you must commit
yourselves wholeheartedly to these commands that I am
giving you today. Repeat them again and again to your
children. Talk about them when you are at home and when
you are on the road, when you are going to bed and when
you are getting up. Tie them to your hands and wear them
on your forehead as reminders. Write them on the doorposts
of your house and on your gates.* Deuteronomy 6:5-9

God's Word is always fresh and never goes out of style.
But did you ever think about decorating your home or
wardrobe with it?

I have read today's verses many times, but until
now I hadn't pondered the reason that Moses instructed
God's people to actually style themselves and their
homes with God's Word. They did not have their own
copies of the Scriptures in their homes, much less multiple versions like we have today. The only way they
could pass down God's promises and directions was by
making these important truths such a part of their daily
lives that they stored them in their hearts and were able
to recite them in their homes.

In the world, fashion continually changes, and society keeps adapting to keep up with the times. God's truth never changes because it doesn't need to! His Word is always relevant and is available to us in countless versions of the Bible as well as being accessible online. His truth will be evident in our homes and in our hearts when we practice it by faith. He doesn't want His truth to remain closed in a book; He wants to use it by His Spirit to style us more like Him.

You and I cannot give out what we do not have. Wherever we are, we cannot talk about the Lord and what He says through Scripture unless we know what it says. God asks us to commit ourselves wholeheartedly to His Word because He is the Word.

● ● ● ● ● ● ● ● ● ●

## LET'S DRESS FOR THE DAY WITH HIS WORD IN OUR HEARTS! CHOOSE A VERSE TO MEMORIZE TODAY. HOW ABOUT THE FIRST SENTENCE IN TODAY'S VERSES FROM DEUTERONOMY ABOVE?

# 79

# The Power of
# This Moment

*Make the most of every opportunity in
these evil days.* Ephesians 5:16

When was the last time you had a professional photograph taken of yourself? Maybe your family gets them taken every fall for an upcoming Christmas card, or perhaps you've had a picture taken recently for work.

Professional photos are great because we have time to primp and prepare beforehand, the photographer shoots us in several poses, and sometimes we can even make clothing changes. When the photographic proofs arrive, we can choose the ones we think look the best. Heaven forbid if we have to start over!

As beautiful as a finished photograph may be, it doesn't usually present a realistic view of everyday life. Life is messy and spontaneous, and we're often thrown curveballs that make redos impossible. And sometimes we just don't look our best on the inside or the outside.

When it comes to living for God and preparing for Jesus' return, we need to make the most of each moment we have left on earth because no one knows the exact time and date when He will come back. We need to be ready as well as to help others be ready too. Although we don't know the timing of that momentous event, we can live life from one candid snapshot to the next, showing Christ's light developing in us. After we're gone, those snapshot memories will serve as a legacy to others that will glorify Him.

I believe that each connection we make with another person provides an opportunity to display an image of Christ's love to him or her. That's how we live out today's verse. The world is filled with images of sin and darkness, and what it really needs to see are images of Christ the Savior, Lord, King, Sustainer, Provider, Refuge, and Friend. Talk about the Power of a moment!

· · · · · · · · · · ·

WHAT CHARACTERISTICS OF GOD WILL YOU SHOW TO A NEEDY WORLD TODAY? ASK HIM TO HELP YOU LEAVE HIS IMAGE EVERYWHERE YOU GO AND THROUGH EVERYTHING YOU SAY IN HIS STRENGTH AND POWER, JUST AS COLOSSIANS 3:17 SAYS.

# 80

## Full Life Even in Suffering

*Then he died, an old man who had
lived a long, full life.* Job 42:17

The entire book of Job addresses suffering, yet I have
laughed out loud at some of the things Job's friends said
to him. Job's circumstances were awful and definitely
not laughable, but some of the comments from his
friends were so blunt I think I laughed in sheer shock.
They sound like something a person might say today.
For example, one man actually called Job a windbag
(Job 15:2)!

Laughing aside, reading this poetic book has caused
me to worship God. What a story of His sovereign
Lordship and constant presence and care over a man
whose heart belonged wholly to God.

Job lost everything. In one day, Job's camels and
oxen were stolen, all his servants were killed, seven thousand sheep and their shepherds were killed by lightning,
and all ten of his children were killed in a cyclone. Then
Job was struck with a terribly painful disease. To make
matters worse, everyone was talking about it, but no one
offered lasting support. Receiving the brunt of gossip
and feeling abandoned in the pain must have felt like

being kicked while he was down. But through all of it, "Job did not sin by blaming God" (Job 1:22).

As believers, we sometimes struggle with the subject of suffering. We ask why, just as Job did. His whole book addresses the dilemma of suffering, and the "arguments" sound familiar today. Let's start asking *who* instead of *why*. God gets the last word, and it is always good, right, and perfect. In Job's life, God sets things right and blesses him more at the end of his life than at the beginning.

You and I will never get the subject of suffering figured out this side of heaven, but we can know without a shadow of a doubt who is in control. All of our suffering is tucked beneath God's outstretched arms as He governs the beginning, the middle, and the end. We can crawl into the arms of the One who truly knows and loves us and wait it out, trusting in His kind, generous, and constant care.

* * * * * * * * * *

WE NEVER HAVE TO KNOW *WHY*; WE JUST NEED
TO KNOW *WHO*. ONLY GOD CAN GIVE US
A FULL LIFE, EVEN IN SUFFERING.

# 81

# Something Good Is Going On

*We know that God causes everything to work together*
*for the good of those who love God and are called*
*according to his purpose for them.* Romans 8:28

Romans 8:28 definitely makes the top ten in my
Precious Personal Promise list. I memorized this verse
as a young Christian, and it has truly given me courage
in every difficult situation. I know for a fact that even if
I can't see any good in my circumstances when I am in
the midst of them, God is working behind the scenes for
my good.

I love going to stage productions. Part of my fascina-
tion is how quickly the stage crew can change scenes.
Everything grows dark for a few moments, and then—
all of a sudden—the curtain opens, the lights come on,
and the audience sees a whole new world!

Whatever scene God's children are in, change is
coming. We can find hope not only in that, but even
more so in His promise that the final scene change will
be phenomenal! Isn't this encouraging? No matter what
happens to us on earth, we will come out ahead in the
end as His children.

Who else can promise gain in loss? Who else can

promise beauty in ugliness? Who else can promise joy in sorrow? Only God!

By dwelling daily on the promise of Romans 8:28, we can encourage ourselves in the Lord, no matter what. Something good is always going on with God.

. . . . . . . . . .

IN THIS WILD WORLD WE LIVE IN, MANY OF US ARE IN TIGHT SPOTS. YOU AND I MAY BE IN ONE RIGHT NOW. WE MUST PULL TOGETHER AND REFUSE TO LET THE ENEMY DISCOURAGE US. I AM SENDING A TIGHT, HOLY HUG TO YOU TODAY. IF YOU BELONG TO GOD IN CHRIST, YOUR BIGGEST BATTLE IS WON. SOMETHING GOOD IS GOING ON IN YOUR LIFE! ASK HIM TO GIVE YOU HOPE TO BELIEVE TODAY.

# 82

# Ultimate Redemption

*Fear not, for I have redeemed you.*  Isaiah 43:1, NKJV

*Redeem* is a big word in the Bible. I looked it up
in my *Scholastic Children's Dictionary*, where the
definition read, "to exchange something for money or
merchandise."

When I was a little girl, my father worked for a
company called Sperry & Hutchinson (S&H), which
gave out green stamps at the grocery store based on the
amount of money you spent. We always supported the
store that gave out green stamps because it supported
Daddy's company, and we loved the rewards.

After shopping, my brother, Bubba, and I would
run home to lick and stick our stamps into little paper
books, excited to watch the books pile up. We were
saving up for something pictured in the prize catalog,
or better yet, we'd go to the actual store where the merchandise was displayed and redeem our green stamp–
filled books for some toy, game, or vacuum cleaner.
(Please, Mama, not the vacuum!) It was so much fun to
collect and save for *free stuff.*

As a child, I had a hard time understanding that
there was a cost involved. That childlike mind-set is
what I believe the Lord would like us to have when He

says, "Fear not, Kim. Fear not, Sweet (insert your name). I have redeemed you." Jesus Christ has purchased our freedom from the bondage of sin, at the ultimate cost to Himself, His blood shed on the cross.

We can't begin to really understand all it cost Him, but because of what Jesus did, we can enjoy freedom from fear. He redeemed us for eternity, and He looks out for us perfectly and practically in this life.

What do you fear? Offer it back to God as a step of faith, thanking Him for buying your freedom and allowing you to enjoy living with childlike trust in Him.

* * * * * * * * * *

THANK GOD TODAY FOR REMOVING OUR FEARS. IF YOU NEED TO RELEASE A FEAR TO HIM RIGHT NOW, PLEASE DO SO. HE HAS REDEEMED YOU AS HIS OWN AT GREAT COST.

# 83

# Ye Olde Crock-Pot

*Thank God! He has made us his captives and continues to lead us along in Christ's triumphal procession. Now he uses us to spread the knowledge of Christ everywhere, like a sweet perfume. Our lives are a Christ-like fragrance rising up to God. But this fragrance is perceived differently by those who are being saved and by those who are perishing. To those who are perishing, we are a dreadful smell of death and doom. But to those who are being saved, we are a life-giving perfume.* 2 Corinthians 2:14-16

Don't you love walking into a home and smelling the aroma of dinner cooking?

When fall brings the first chill in the air, I can't wait to pull out the old Crock-Pot that my grandmother Nana gave us as a wedding present. The convenience of throwing in a variety of ingredients in the morning and knowing that a no-fuss meal will be ready at dinnertime makes my day! And don't you wish your drop-in visitors would come on a Crock-Pot day and be so impressed with the mouth-watering aroma drifting through your home, instead of on a day you purposely planned to stay in your pajamas and were going to heat up leftovers?

God tells all believers that we smell like Christ to each other and to Him, because Christ's Spirit in His children is a scent that attracts us to each other. We recognize His fragrance in others because we know Him in ourselves. He is a unifier among His people, the fragrance of life that we share in Him. God's scent either draws or repels others, depending on whether their hearts are open to Him. Just as fragrances are undeniably pleasant or distasteful, His aroma carries the message of death to those still in opposition to Him.

As believers, living true to God's Word and in obedience to Him, we diffuse His aroma around others, and He always smells wonderful. Even those who don't readily recognize the true Source of the aroma may be curious about His signature scent of salvation, truth, and grace.

• • • • • • • • • •

THE NEXT TIME THE AROMA FROM THE KITCHEN WELCOMES US HOME, LET'S BE REMINDED THAT WE SMELL LIKE CHRIST TO GOD, AND THAT SMELLS GOOD! PLAN TO SHARE A MEAL WITH SOMEONE THIS WEEK.

# 84

# Dreams I Wanted to Keep

*I lie awake thinking of you, meditating
on you through the night.*
Psalm 63:6

I agree with David's words in this psalm. There have been many nights when my restless mind has been calmed by thinking about God. It seems fitting to spend time thinking of our Creator as often as we can.

One middle-school morning, my daughter was really hard to awaken from sweet slumber. I tried my usual wake-up song (which is a slight variation from the original)—"Good morning, good morning, you slept the whole night through; good morning, good morning to you"—but it wasn't doing the trick.

When Kali finally opened her eyes, I asked her why she was a real sleepyhead this particular morning. Her answer melted my heart. "I was having dreams I wanted to keep."

*Dreams I Wanted to Keep* sounded like a great book title to me! Later in the day, I pondered the words. A personal relationship with the God of the whole universe is not a dream. It is a reality. When we awaken every morning surrounded by the Lord's presence in this

earthly life, our connection with Him is "for keeps"—
now and for all eternity.

Jesus Christ's Holy Spirit is our constant companion
who lives inside every believer. We can live in hopeful
anticipation of seeing His face when He calls us home
to heaven. In the meantime, we must carry His truths
close to our hearts and meditate on them always, day
and night.

To be honest, Jesus is the greatest dream come true
and the most precious One we can keep and offer to
others.

* * * * * * * * * *

WHEN WE WAKE UP IN THE MORNING, LET'S
THANK THE LORD JESUS CHRIST THAT HE IS NOT A
DREAM! HE IS "FOR KEEPS" NOW AND FOREVER!

# 85

# All in God's Hands

*No one can come to Me unless the Father who*
*sent Me draws him.*  John 6:44, NKJV

Jesus draws people! This truth frees me, relaxes me, comforts me, and makes me want to jump up and down with joy.

You see, I love people, and I want everyone to know Jesus so they will have real, priceless hope, even in the heartaches of life. But I'm so relieved that it isn't up to me at all to change people's hearts—Jesus draws people to Himself.

I cannot do anything to change someone's heart one iota to desire God. When I finally realized this fact and that I was not responsible to give a "perfect" gospel presentation or be the perfect example of a Christian in order for someone to come to Christ, I relaxed. This was a huge burden off my shoulders.

Now, please do not misunderstand me. I am not relaxed about caring. I care about people. I care where people will spend eternity; I want to be in heaven with everyone. I want people to know Christ, not just because their eternal destination is at stake, but also because I cannot imagine experiencing the troubles in this life without relying on a loving and patient Savior. He never keeps any record of my wrongs (1 Corinthians 13:5) and is an ever-present help in trouble (Psalm 46:1, NIV).

Knowing that all the power for change and redemption is in the hands of God is so freeing. We can relax in God's faithfulness and provision, believing He will give us all we need to do what He wants us to do or say. He promised us that His Holy Spirit will reside in our hearts and will reflect Him to others in this hurting world as we go through our daily responsibilities.

Whew! Go God!

GOD DOES ALL THE HARD WORK IN PEOPLE'S HEARTS. LET'S ASK HIM TO GIVE US SENSITIVITY TO HOW HE WANTS US TO REACH OUT TO OTHERS WITH HIS GOOD NEWS.

# 86

# Good Medicine

*A cheerful heart is good medicine, but a broken spirit saps a person's strength.* Proverbs 17:22

When I was going through chemotherapy, I wanted to reassure my daughter of God's kind care for me even when I looked different—without any hair, eyelashes, or eyebrows. (Boy, did I ever learn some new makeup skills!)

I explained to her that the chemotherapy was "good medicine," and losing my hair was a sign that the medicine was working, killing the good cells as well as the bad cancer cells. Also, I assured her of my gratefulness to God for all the doctors and nurses that He had provided to give me the medicine.

But just as surely as there is good medicine, there is also bad medicine. Some medicines can immediately offer lifesaving benefits. Others, if used incorrectly, can cause death. As important as it is to have the correct medicine for our physical bodies, it's more critical to know what we need for our spiritual health.

How in the world can we call in a prescription for a joyful heart? By obediently remaining in Jesus' love (John 15:9-11) and taking our needs to God in Jesus' name (John 16:24). Now, *that's* good medicine! I have never had a cheerful heart when I've disobeyed God's Word. I have never had a cheerful heart if I have refused to forgive someone or if I have lost my temper and failed to make it right. However, I have experienced joy when I have lived by God's Word and entrusted my needs to Him.

True joy comes from living in close fellowship with the Lord, which includes obeying and trusting Him. We cannot manufacture this "good medicine" on our own. It comes from a personal relationship with Jesus Christ.

. . . . . . . . . .

WE CAN KEEP A CHEERFUL, JOYFUL HEART
IN OUR "GOOD MEDICINE" CABINETS BY
BEING OBEDIENT TO CHRIST'S COMMANDS
AND TRUSTING HIM WITH OUR NEEDS.

# 87

# How Fun Is This?

*Give as freely as you have received!* Matthew 10:8

Nothing sparks giving like receiving! What is the first thing we want to do when someone gives us something? We want to return the gesture, right after we say thank you! We often think about the sender and choose something that would be meaningful and special to that person.

The Lord inspires me by example more than anyone on this earth. If I am struggling in any way and I hear God's viewpoint from His Word, I am inspired by His Spirit to move closer to His way of thinking. The times I have been prompted in my spirit but failed to give are moments I regret. I can't think of one time I wished I hadn't given.

In today's verse the Lord is instructing us to give as freely as we have received. It's a practice that I have purposed in my heart to follow, especially since I get so much enjoyment out of the process. I look to God's immeasurable example. Two thousand years ago He gave us quite the inspiration to follow when He gave us His Son, Jesus—the ultimate gift.

As believers in Christ, we have received salvation—a gift that can't be topped. But He also has given us the power of His Holy Spirit and His provision of love, joy, peace, and comfort even in the midst of the difficulties and heartaches of life. Oh, how much we have received from His abundant love! There is no other response but to follow His example and make the choice to freely give to others our time, talents, and treasures.

"When you give to someone in need, don't let your left hand know what your right hand is doing. Give your gifts in private, and your Father, who sees everything, will reward you" (Matthew 6:3-4).

· · · · · · · · · · ·

GIVE SOMETHING TODAY THAT WARRANTS NOTHING IN RETURN, EVER, AND DO NOT TELL ANYONE. THAT GIFT COUNTS AS GIVING DIRECTLY TO GOD. HE SEES, AND HIS NOTICE IS ALL THAT MATTERS!

# 88

# In His Arms

*Praise the Lord; praise God our savior! For each day he carries us in his arms. Our God is a God who saves! The Sovereign LORD rescues us from death.* Psalm 68:19-20

Each day the Lord, the God of all comfort, carries us in His arms. Imagine that. Our Sovereign God—who is the Lord of Heaven's Armies (Isaiah 48:2) and the Creator of all things—is tender toward His children.

I picture His love every Sunday at church when, right before the closing song, a small curly-haired toddler comes bounding through one of the rear doors into the sanctuary. Bubbling with delight, she runs down the aisle to her sweet mother, who stoops low with wide-open arms to snatch her up! I worship every time I have the privilege of seeing this precious sight—

> because I see Jesus, stooped low to embrace us;
> because He walked on this dirty earth around dirty
>     people, but made us clean when He died on the
>     cross for you and me;
> because Jesus literally rescued us from death.

Not only does Jesus stoop low, but His arms are wide open just like they were when they were stretched out on the cross. You may have heard that body language makes up 90 percent of our communication. Well, Jesus communicates 100 percent of His abounding love with His arms wide open, calling out a welcome: "Come to me, all of you who are weary and carry heavy burdens, and I will give you rest" (Matthew 11:28). When we run to those holy arms, the God of all the earth scoops us up and carries us through sickness, grief, loss, unemployment, and any other pain. Through it *all* He carries us!

. . . . . . . . . .

EACH DAY THE LORD CARRIES US IN HIS ARMS. MAKE TIME TO CURL UP FOR DELIBERATE REST TODAY—EVEN IF IT IS ONLY FIFTEEN MINUTES. IMAGINE YOURSELF IN THE LORD'S ARMS AND REVEL IN HIS LOVE.

# 89

## Changed

*This same Good News that came to you is going out
all over the world. It is bearing fruit everywhere by
changing lives, just as it changed your lives from
the day you first heard and understood the truth
about God's wonderful grace.* Colossians 1:6

Over the years I have appreciated what I've learned
from reading women's magazines—skills such as how to
arrange furniture, pick out a paint color, make a fruit
smoothie, or apply brow powder. But honestly, nothing
major in my life was ever really changed by reading
a magazine.

On the other hand, *I* am changed as I grow to know
Christ better each day through His Word. He promises that His infallible Word always produces fruit and
accomplishes all He wants. It prospers everywhere He
sends it (Isaiah 55:11). When I get a daily dose of what
God has to say and walk by faith in His strength, He
works His life-changing transformation in me.

I love to try new products and change things around
from time to time. Getting a new chair for the living
room adds a fresh look to our home. A new lipstick
color rejuvenates me. But there are other changes that
unsettle me, especially if they are unexpected and take

me through tough times or require me to step far out of my comfort zone.

But God created us with His heart for greater purposes beyond our own plans. Living for Him means having an openness to let Him do things differently in us. If He knows our current path doesn't lead to His best for us, He may reroute us another way. We can trust that His changes are always for our best as He leads us on an adventure that will glorify Him.

When we allow Him in His wonderful grace to have His way in us, we are assured of a life that fits who He created us to be.

• • • • • • • • • • •

LET'S THANK THE LORD TODAY FOR CHANGING US
AND MAKING US READY FOR HIS GREATER PURPOSE
FOR US. WE CAN TRUST HIM TO BE THERE WHEN
WE ARE STEERED OUT OF OUR COMFORT ZONES.

# 90

# This Is My Lord

*I love you, LORD; you are my strength. The LORD is my rock, my fortress, and my savior; my God is my rock, in whom I find protection.* Psalm 18:1-2

When we pass a particular church in our neighborhood, even though it is not where we attend, at least one member in our family usually says in a childlike voice, "This is *my* church!" We are imitating four-year-old Jack, one of the precious children Kali babysits. Every time the two of them were in the car headed to the playground or another fun excursion and passed Jack's church, he owned it!

This morning as I read the wonderful words in the first two verses of Psalm 18, I am reminded of just how personal our relationship is to our Lord. Read the verses out loud with me right now, emphasizing the word *my* every time it is used:

I love You, Lord:
*My* Strength, *My* Rock,
*My* Fortress, *My* Savior,
*My* God.

Because we are His, He is ours! We can pray about any need we have, any emotional turmoil we are experiencing in our hearts, because we have His ears and eyes and heart and Holy Spirit 24/7.

"Lord, I feel weak, emotionally and physically today, but You are *my* strength!"

"Lord, I feel like I am melting in a puddle—but You are *my* Rock, immovable and unchanging!"

"Lord, I feel attacked, but You are *my* Fortress— You surround me. Nothing can come in and out of my life unless it has gone past You."

"Lord, I feel like life is a daily battle with circumstances only You can really see and understand. You know all that is happening, and I always win with You because You are *my* Savior!"

"You are *my* God!"

. . . . . . . . . .

### TAKE A MINUTE ALONE TODAY AND READ THE VERSES OUT LOUD TO GOD.

# 91

## Seeing in the Fog

*We live by faith, not by sight.* 2 Corinthians 5:7, NIV

I am almost breathless. God's creation is spectacular! My "so excited face" is on right now as I am literally sitting in a cloud! No, I am not in an airplane. I am outside early in the morning, sitting on a balcony surrounded by mountains.

Just a minute ago I was gazing at the valley and small town below, getting ready to read my Bible while anticipating a slow and restful week with my family on summer vacation. I was gazing at the tops of the mountains and pieces of blue sky peeking between the clouds, wondering if it was going to rain. Then all of a sudden, I couldn't see a thing! I was totally enveloped by a cloudy fog.

I cannot see the church steeple, cannot see the forest, cannot see one mountain peak because of the clouds surrounding me. But I can still hear. I hear the sound of a gushing waterfall. A few more seconds pass before it dawns on me that I cannot see God, either! But I know He is here just as sure as that mountain is sitting behind the cloud. Paradoxically, it is probably one of the clearest visual pictures I have had personally of what it means to walk by faith and not by sight!

"Lord, right now, my circumstances are a bit cloudy, and I do not know what is ahead, but I do know that You do. And as sure as those mountains are still behind the clouds, You are behind every cloudy circumstance in my life. You never leave, Lord."

Our circumstances can change abruptly, without warning, and leave us feeling blinded about what to do next. Many times we cannot see what is behind our situation or what unknowns lie in front of us, but we can still hear God in His Word. I hear Him in this Bible beside me. I hear Him saying right now that one day my faith will become sight.

. . . . . . . . . . .

IT'S OKAY THAT WE CANNOT SEE GOD. WE CAN HEAR HIM AND KNOW THAT HE IS PRESENT WITH US BECAUSE HE SAYS SO OVER AND OVER IN HIS WORD. LET'S PRAY NOW THAT HE WILL HELP US TRUST HIM SO MUCH THAT WE FIND PEACE IN THE FOG.

# 92

# Genuine Gratitude

*[David] refused to drink it. Instead, he poured it
out as an offering to the LORD. "The LORD forbid
that I should drink this!" he exclaimed. "This water
is as precious as the blood of these men who risked
their lives to bring it to me."* 2 Samuel 23:16-17

What would our world look like without genuine
gratitude and sacrifice? When I start to complain, I need
a shot of gratitude instead of gripe-itude. Sometimes I
think I am going to pop in gratefulness to God for all
He has done for me and how He has used others to give
so generously to our family.

Do you ever feel at a loss about how to thank people
whom God has placed in your life, knowing that you
can never begin to convey the fullness of your thankful
heart? You feel *so* much gratitude, but the problem is,
you don't know how to express it adequately. You know
that nothing you have accomplished has happened
because of you alone.

God uses the body of Christ to fulfill His purposes
on earth. God has specific jobs for each of us to do.
Nothing happens in our own strength, and certainly our
growth in gratitude does not happen apart from God's
power in us.

Indulge me for a minute. Just for this devotion, I want to adapt the words from 2 Samuel 23:9 (KJV) describing David's "mighty" men to describe the "mighty sweet men *and women*" God has placed in my life. When David was thirsty, three of his mighty men broke through the Philistine lines and drew water from the well near the gate of Bethlehem (where David was born) and carried it back to their leader. "But he [David] refused to drink it. Instead, he poured it out as an offering to the LORD" (2 Samuel 23:16). What I long to do is pour out my little cracked teacup filled with sugar cubes as an offering to the Lord to show my gratitude too.

We can all show genuine gratitude to God by purposely pouring out everything. You and I need to rest in the knowledge that God sees our gratefulness. It does not matter if anyone notices what we do to give back. When we offer ourselves wholeheartedly to God, our gratitude blesses Him, us, and others around us.

* * * * * * * * * * *

SERVING OTHERS SACRIFICIALLY IS ONE WAY TO POUR OUT GRATITUDE TO OUR GRACIOUS GOD.

# 93

# Fresh, Bubbling Spring

*Those who drink the water I give will never be
thirsty again. It becomes a fresh, bubbling spring
within them, giving them eternal life.* John 4:14

Over the years, I've learned the benefits of drinking
water. Not only does it decrease my appetite, but it keeps
me from being thirsty at the end of a long day. And it
really does hydrate my dry skin, too. The only downside
is that drinking sixty-four ounces of water daily is not an
easy thing for me to do, but I'll keep trying!

When it comes to Jesus, the Living Water, I'm not a
sipper—I'm a guzzler, and I want to guzzle all day long!
Jesus makes it clear to us in Scripture that when we
receive Him, He will produce a fresh, bubbling spring
in us.

The story in John 4:1-42 is one of my favorites. Jesus
is weary and thirsty after journeying all day, and while
His disciples go into town to buy food, He sits down
at Jacob's well. A woman comes to get water, and Jesus
asks her for a drink. She is startled because she knows
that a Jewish man normally wouldn't talk to an outcast
like her. But not so with Jesus. He knows everything
about her, but He still offers Himself to her as the Living

Water. The woman accepts Jesus' gift, goes back to town, and tells everyone she meets what happened. Because of her testimony, many others believe and receive Jesus too.

Wow! I can't imagine the excitement in town that day or the life changes that her newfound joy and salvation prompted in her.

The Lord loves us so! He is the only one who can keep our spirit fresh and bubbling with His life in us, regardless of how the world's troubles threaten to dry us up and scorch our tender souls.

Doesn't it sound more appealing to have a fresh spring in our hearts than a stagnant pool? Life often leaves us spiritually thirsty, but when we are hydrated by Him, we can thrive even in desert situations. When we drink daily from our Living Water supply, hearing His voice above all others, we can pour out His freshness to a thirsty world.

. . . . . . . . . .

## FRESH AND BUBBLING? LIFE-QUENCHING? I'LL TAKE IT! WON'T YOU?

# 94

# Songs of Confidence

*My heart is confident in you, O God; my heart is confident. No wonder I can sing your praises! Wake up, my heart! Wake up, O lyre and harp! I will wake the dawn with my song.* Psalm 57:7-8

*Psalm* means "song," and even though we do not know the original tune of Psalm 57 and may not have greeted the dawn with a song today, we can sing along with David about our confidence in Christ.

Why is it possible to have so much confidence in God? Well, not only has He delivered us from our enemies of sin, death, and the devil because of the victory Christ won on the cross, but we have a loving refuge in Him in the midst of upsetting circumstances. We have a Defender and a Conqueror who has unlimited capabilities to fight on our behalf. He wants us to be as confident in Him as He is in Himself.

In the introductory note for this psalm to the choir director, it says, "A psalm of David, regarding the time he fled from Saul and went into the cave. To be sung to the tune 'Do Not Destroy!'" David was fleeing for his life, finally admitting to God how weary he was from his distress (verse 6). If David, the man after God's own heart, became weary from distress, we can go to God to renew our confident faith too.

Going to God and taking hold of His peace is such a privilege. We must choose to put our confidence in Christ because He sees the before and after and ever after of every event in our lives.

"Lord, You loved David in his distress and You love me in mine! You know I'm upset about _____ (fill in the blank), but I trust You, Lord. I feel weary. I am tired of hiding, running, and complaining. I have You as my confidence builder. I open my heart to You right now."

* * * * * * * * * *

SHOUT OUT WITH ME WHATEVER DISTRESS YOU ARE FACING TODAY. THEN COMBAT THAT CIRCUMSTANCE WITH CHRIST'S SURE CONFIDENCE, WHICH IS RIGHTFULLY OURS IF WE BELONG TO HIM! READ EPHESIANS 3:12 TO SEE WHAT THAT CONFIDENCE COMPELS US TO DO.

# 95

# Always Connected

*I am convinced that nothing can ever separate us from
God's love. Neither death nor life, neither angels nor
demons, neither our fears for today nor our worries about
tomorrow—not even the powers of hell can separate
us from God's love. No power in the sky above or in
the earth below—indeed, nothing in all creation will
ever be able to separate us from the love of God that is
revealed in Christ Jesus our Lord.* Romans 8:38-39

Before my beautiful, naturally curly-haired, redheaded
mother (her hair reminded me of Lucille Ball's) went to
be with the Lord, she told me she got exasperated with
long phone-recording prompts. One time she had tried
several times to reach a real person to take care of essen-
tial business. After hearing "This call may be monitored
for quality assurance," she left her own message: "I sure
hope so, because I have something to tell you!" I wish I
could hear her say those words now so I could laugh out
loud again in her actual presence.

Meditating on the verses from Romans 8 that are
quoted above feels like God is pulling us close and
saying, "I have something to tell you: Nothing can
separate you from My love!" You and I can be encouraged, no matter who or what we are separated from, that

*absolutely nothing* can separate us from God through Christ Jesus.

His quality assurance is so reliable that we never get a recording when we call on Him. We never have a dropped call with Him, and His signal strength is amazing—it's everywhere! He promises His constant presence and immediate attention. He even knows before we do when and in what way we'll need Him.

You know what else? Staying connected is even more important to Him than it is to us. He chose long ago to rescue us, and He's not willing to ever give us up. Our connection with Him is as secure as He is—perfectly so.

Talk about great service. God can't be beat!

* * * * * * * * * *

YOU KNOW THAT CONCERN THAT'S BEEN SOUNDING A BUSY SIGNAL IN YOUR THOUGHTS? CALL ON GOD AND TELL HIM ABOUT IT. THERE'S NO NEED TO LEAVE A MESSAGE—HE'S AVAILABLE AND HE ALWAYS ANSWERS, HIS WAY, HIS TIME. HE GOT THE MESSAGE FOR SURE, AND OH, HE HAS NO NEED FOR CALLER ID, EITHER— HE ALREADY KNEW YOU'D BE CALLING.

# 96

## History with God

> "You are my witnesses, O Israel!" says the LORD.
> "You are my servant. You have been chosen to know
> me, believe in me, and understand that I alone am
> God. There is no other God—there never has been, and
> there never will be. I, yes I, am the LORD, and there
> is no other Savior. . . . From eternity to eternity I am
> God. No one can snatch anyone out of my hand. No
> one can undo what I have done." Isaiah 43:10-11, 13

History was not my best subject in school. But ever
since I began reading the Bible, I have become an avid
history student.

Seeing God care for His people over and over again
despite their continual disobedience has drawn me to
worship such a patient, loving, merciful Lord.

God cares for His people from eternity to eternity,
as only the one true God can. He reminds all of us that
there is no other God—never has been, never will be!

The history of Israel recorded for us in the Bible is
our heritage too. Through His people, God showed a
lost world that He alone is God. Today's verses are just
a taste of the precious relationship God has with His
people—then, now, and forever. He claims us and gives
us a place of belonging and hope in Him.

"But now, O Jacob, listen to the LORD who created you. O Israel, the one who formed you says, 'Do not be afraid, for I have ransomed you. I have called you by name; you are mine'" (Isaiah 43:1). When we accept the Lord's gift of salvation, we are His forever. In fact, He tells us that He called us by name—such an intimate, knowledgeable, and personal act on His part. He says no one can undo that fact: we are His and He is ours.

⬤ ⬤ ⬤ ⬤ ⬤ ⬤ ⬤ ⬤ ⬤ ⬤

WE HAVE A HISTORY. WE HAVE A HISTORY WITH GOD THROUGH JESUS CHRIST! PLEASE READ ALL OF ISAIAH 43 IN WONDER AND WORSHIP OF GOD. LET'S REJOICE THAT OUR HISTORY WITH GOD WILL CONTINUE THROUGHOUT OUR FUTURE WITH HIM.

# 97

# Best Friend

*You are my friends if you do what I command.* John 15:14

Do you have a best friend? There aren't too many relationships as sweet as those shared by best friends. Maybe you can name several who have filled that role for you throughout your life. Isn't it amazing that we can all share the same Best Friend, Jesus?

When I read a verse like the one for today, it makes me think what it must have been like to walk this earth as a friend of Jesus. The disciples were His companions, and He was always teaching them what it meant to be His friend. He knew all that was coming and how it would affect them, so He encouraged them to follow His lead. His words of caring direction showed how deep His love was for each of them.

Jesus was fully human, and He had best friends too. Of course, He chose His disciple friends wisely! If I were to guess which of them He'd call a best friend, I'd choose John. I call their twosome friendship "The Special Js."

John wrote about his firsthand experience with Jesus in the Gospel of John, followed by three very personal "sticky notes"—1, 2, and 3 John. John was known as the beloved disciple (John 13:23; 20:2), and he was the man Jesus entrusted with the care of His mother, Mary, as He was dying (John 19:26-27). John also outran Peter to Jesus' tomb (John 20:2-4) because he was so anxious to see what had happened to his Best Friend.

And how precious it is that Jesus' best earthly friend was the one God chose to write Jesus' words in Revelation, the last book of the Bible, to encourage us and prepare us for His final coming and to offer us a glimpse of what's ahead. John's life of obedience to Jesus' mission after He ascended to heaven attests to the fact that their friendship was genuine.

I love these examples of how personal Jesus is to His followers—He loves building friendships with us. He knows we need Him as a Best Friend, and He wants to help us all discover that special relationship with Him.

* * * * * * * * * *

LET'S SEEK THE COMPANY OF OUR BEST FRIEND AND SPEND TIME WITH THOSE WHO SHARE THAT SAME FRIENDSHIP WITH HIM. ONLY IN CHRIST CAN WE ALL HAVE THE VERY SAME BEST FRIEND.

# 98

# Sweet Ps

*I will study your commandments and*
*reflect on your ways. I will delight in your*
*decrees and not forget your word.*
Psalm 119:15-16

Psalm 119 is the longest psalm in the Bible, and as much as I would like to include it in its entirety here, there isn't enough room! These two verses from the psalm are great motivators—I don't want to miss a day of hearing God's voice through the pages of Scripture. How in the world can I delight in His decrees if I don't know them? How can I reflect on His ways if I do not know what God is like? How can I hear God's voice above all others if I don't recognize it?

In all honesty, I can't delight in something I don't understand or value simply because I'm told to do so. Our delight for something or someone is a gut-level response, a natural overflow of the heart. When I read God's Word daily, I come to know and love Him, which leads me to delight in what He says—just as today's Scripture says.

I don't ever want to forget His Word. But because I have an imperfect memory and a tendency to question and wonder, I need reminders of all the reasons why

He's so worthy of my delight. Here are five Sweet P tips to cheer us all along in God's ways:

1. Prioritize. Let's make knowing God a priority. Knowing God is the purpose of reading His Word, which is accessible to everyone.
2. Pick a comfy spot in your home where you do not see the dishes and the laundry. Face a window or go outside. Have your Bible and a cup of coffee or tea handy.
3. Pray. Prayer is just talking to God: "Lord, will You teach me about Yourself when I open Your Word? Will You teach me about myself, and show me ways to put what You say into practice?"
4. Plunge in. Do not be afraid. He talks to all His people through His Word.
5. Put some sticky notes near your Bible to mark places that you want to return to as you flip back and forth through His truths.

· · · · · · · · · ·

PLEASE JOIN ME IN DELIGHTING DAILY IN THE LORD'S DECREES.

# 99

# Help Yourself to Me, Lord!

*My old self has been crucified with Christ. It is no
longer I who live, but Christ lives in me. So I live in
this earthly body by trusting in the Son of God, who
loved me and gave himself for me.* Galatians 2:20

I love what Oswald Chambers says about this verse in
his classic devotional book, *My Utmost for His Highest.*
During a lecture to his students at Bible Training
College in Clapham Common, London, he said, "This
college is an organization that is not worth anything.
It is not academic; it is for nothing else but for God to
help Himself to lives. Is He going to help Himself to us,
or are we taken up with our conception of what we are
going to be?"

*Wow!* My heart replies back: *Lord, help Yourself to me!
Take seconds, thirds, fourths, and fifths!*

Isn't it wonderful that we will never be sent back to
the kitchen, banned from sitting at God's banquet table
to feast on His perpetual potluck dinner prepared just
for us in Christ Jesus? It's a perfect dinner spread out
on white linen tablecloths, with real silver and gorgeous
china plates—all God's best that He has offered to us.
He wants us to help ourselves to His presence, too!

We may bring a fancy dish or a simple one because we all have faith of different sizes, and we have different styles of expressing our faith and worshiping Him. He delights in variety because it is evident throughout His creation. Just as no two people are alike and each snowflake is different, so it is with our unique places and contributions at His banquet table.

Yes, He loves variety, but He wants the same wholehearted devotion from each one of us. He wants all of us to hear and respond, "Help Yourself to our lives, Lord!"

* * * * * * * * * *

IN WHAT WAY CAN WE SAY, "LORD, HELP YOURSELF! HELP YOURSELF, LORD, TO US"? PERHAPS WE CAN DEMONSTRATE HIS LOVE TO SOMEONE THIS WEEK. MAYBE WE COULD LET HIS CHARACTER SHINE BRIGHTLY IN OUR RESPONSES TO OTHERS. OR MAYBE WE COULD ASK HIM WHETHER HE HAS A NEW DIRECTION FOR OUR LIVES.

# 100

# Living the "Seek" Life

*Solomon, my son, learn to know the God of your
ancestors intimately. Worship and serve him with your
whole heart and a willing mind. For the LORD sees
every heart and knows every plan and thought. If you
seek him, you will find him.* 1 Chronicles 28:9

This verse is an excerpt from a serious man-to-man,
father-and-son talk. King David is close to death, and
these are some of his last words of advice to his son,
Solomon. We know David was far from perfect as a
husband, father, and king. But he led a *seek* life and is
known as a man after God's own heart (Acts 13:22).

As a child, I always loved playing hide-and-seek.
But when it comes to God, I wonder sometimes if
I'm searching well for Him. I know it's impossible to
hide from Him, but what does it look like to actively
*seek* Him?

Today's verse in 1 Chronicles reminds me of the
greatest commandment: "Love the LORD your God
with all your heart, all your soul, and all your mind"
(Matthew 22:37). It's a great verse to meditate on
when we want to learn what it means to seek the Lord.
Seeking is assertive, and if you are seeking something,
you initiate action, instead of waiting around for

things to happen. We can personalize this verse with our own names as our heavenly Father speaks to us through His Word (fill your name in the blanks): "My daughter (my son), _____, learn to know Me, the God of your ancestors, intimately. Worship and serve Me, _____, with your whole heart and a willing mind. For I see your heart and know every plan and thought. If you seek Me, _____, you will find Me."

Living the *seek* life includes reading God's Word to know Him more. We can't help but fall in love with God the more we know Him because of who He is. He is all-perfect, all-loving, kind, just, merciful, and gracious. As we spend time in His presence, we take on His heart. Like King David, we can be people after God's heart.

● ● ● ● ● ● ● ● ● ●

ASK GOD TO GROW YOUR LOVE FOR HIM MORE DEEPLY AS YOU SEEK HIM THROUGH HIS WORD. HE WILL GIVE US WISDOM WHEN WE LIVE THE *SEEK* LIFE.

# 101

# The Celebration of All Celebrations

*Blessed are those who are invited to the wedding feast of the Lamb.* Revelation 19:9

Here is one invitation we do not want to miss! No matter how young or old, heavy-laden or carefree we are, this invitation is ours for the taking. Because Jesus was always saying, "Come" (Matthew 11:28), we can extend the same invitation to others and introduce them to Jesus, the Lamb of God. This is worth spreading the news about! The invitation list is all-inclusive—no one is left out.

Remember what it was like when someone at school was having a birthday party but not every child in the class was invited? If you didn't receive an invitation, it felt awful to know that something was going on and you were not included.

The invitation to the wedding feast referred to in today's verse is an invitation to everyone! It isn't just any old gathering either. It's the premier event of all time and beyond—the wedding feast that will finally celebrate the reunion of Jesus, the Lamb, with His bride, the church— believers in Christ.

The invitation is open until Jesus returns to gather

His own for the journey home. He desires everyone to give an RSVP of "Yes!" and then spread the word about His coming back. Although we cannot RSVP for other guests, Jesus is delighted when they respond to Him with their own personal RSVP of believing faith.

We need to tell others that they have been invited personally by Jesus! If they only check their hearts carefully, they will see His personal welcome waiting there.

We are blessed by this invitation, and we can do our part to encourage others to join us when we share with them the meaning of the wedding feast.

• • • • • • • • • •

LET'S SHARE THE EXCITEMENT ABOUT THE FEAST JESUS IS PREPARING FOR HIS WEDDING PARTY! HELP OTHERS REALIZE THEY'RE INVITED, AND THEY CAN'T AFFORD TO MISS IT. READ REVELATION 19:6-9 FOR A GLIMPSE OF THE BEST OF ALL WEDDING CELEBRATIONS.

*Dear Sweet Reader,*

*You may know Kim Newlen as an author, a speaker, or a friend. I was blessed to call her Mom. For twenty-two years, I watched her model grace and encourage others through the gospel. Mom would often be up before sunrise with God's Word and a cup of coffee or tea. She called it "Purr and Praise Time," with our cat, Fluffy, snuggled up in her lap next to her Bible and devotionals. The pages of her Bible were well worn and had scribbled notes filling the margins, some of which were probably ideas for these devotions! For as long as I can remember, Mom never missed a day in the Word.*

*Consider these devotions as journal entries of my mom's love story with her best friend, our Savior Jesus Christ. These stories expose strength amidst struggles and joy amidst pain, as Mom strove to honor God's purpose for her life. Even during her two-time battle with breast cancer, she trusted in God's plan, saying, "God is sovereign over all of this."*

*Mom's faithful walk with the Lord has uplifted my soul and encouraged my heart. And that is my hope and prayer for you—that you would draw nearer to the God who comforts and heals and protects, the God who encourages and overcomes. The One who gives us this promise in one of my* mom's favorite verses: "In the world you will have tribulation; but be of good cheer, I have overcome the world" (John 16:33, NKJV).

Your sister in Christ,

*Kali* ☺

P.S. Mom liked to sign her name with a smiley face (she called it "smiley faith"), and now I do it too! Don't forget . . . BSSYP! (Be Sweet & Say Your Prayers).

# About the Author

Kim Newlen (1957–2014) believed that God's truth goes together with fun and faithfulness, which inspired her to found Sweet Monday, a ministry which began in her living room in 1995 with the mission of *reaching out to women one sweet invitation at a time for Christ.* The international nonprofit organization continues, in memory of her heartfelt desire to train women in creative evangelism. Although Kim is now in her heavenly home, her legacy is one of laughter, love, and joy that could only come from her Father above. Kim spent time in God's Word daily, hearing His voice through Scripture and seeing evidence of His loving care in her life with her husband, Mark, her daughter, Kali, and her faithful friends.

**Sweet Monday** is creative evangelism that "reaches out to women one sweet invitation at a time for Christ." Women laugh a lot, learn from each other, and leave with a simple introduction to Jesus Christ. Sweet Monday is also a homegrown, tiny tool that God is using in a BIG way to connect women to each other and Himself.

❤❤❤❤❤❤❤❤

Visit www.sweetmonday.org to learn more!

CP0677

Sweet and simple moments
to revive your spirit—
*every day of the year*

978-1-4143-7332-4

In *The One Year Sweet and Simple Moments with God Devotional*,
Kim Newlen encourages us all to take a sweet and simple moment to
be still with God every day. Filled with heart-lightening insights and
inspiration, these devotions will help you make every moment count through
spending time with the One who can carry your burdens best.

CP1006

# Discover the blessings
## GOD HAS WAITING FOR YOU

*Beautiful Blessings from God*

FROM GOD

978-1-4964-1311-6

*Beautiful Blessings from God* is an inspiring and enriching devotional that will show you how to confidently walk God's way and experience His breakthrough blessings in your life. These eloquent daily readings by award-winning author Patricia Raybon will help you embark on the pathway to God's best for you—today and every day. (Adapted from *The One Year God's Great Blessings Devotional.*)

CP1069